*The LNER
2-8-2 and 2-6-2
Classes*

The LNER
2-8-2 and 2-6-2
Classes

J. F. CLAY and
J. CLIFFE

LONDON

IAN ALLAN

First published 1973

ISBN 0 7110 0427 7

© Ian Allan 1973

Published by Ian Allan Ltd., Shepperton, Surrey
and printed in the United Kingdom by A. Wheaton & Co., Exeter

Contents

Preface

There were more ways than one of building a successful steam locomotive. The late Sir Nigel Gresley believed that the best way for his railway was to build a number of classes of big engines with wide fireboxes and three cylinders. He never shrank from building a very small class of a few engines to cover one special operational problem. There were other ways of dealing with the situation and other engineers on other railways also achieved success, but it cannot be denied that the performance of the Gresley locomotives raised the prestige of the LNER to a position second to none in this country. While it would be true to say that he achieved his greatest success with his Pacifics, the A4s especially, the various 2-8-2 and 2-6-2 classes were machines of great interest and historical significance.

It has been the aim of the writers of this book to tell the story of these engines against the general background of contemporary economics and against the record of 2-8-2 and 2-6-2 engines in world history. It is a story of both success and disappointment which we have tried to tell with realism. In doing this we are aware of the fact that we may offend protagonists of both the pro-Gresley and anti-Gresley schools of thought. We submit, however, that a fair summary of evidence has been presented.

Our task in finding a factual basis for the story of the Gresley 2-8-2 and 2-6-2 classes has been made easier by the help of P. J. Coster, who has made available the results of his researches made for a series of articles published in the *Journal of the Stephenson Locomotive Society*. Not only has he interviewed a number of former LNER locomotive engineers, but more recently he has enjoyed the privilege of discussing the performance of No 2001 *Cock o' the North* on test in France with André Chapelon, the greatest locomotive engineer of the second quarter of the 20th Century. We are also grateful for the help of P. H. V. Banyard, H. A. Gamble, G. Goslin, Gp Capt J. N. C. Law and K. R. Phillips. We thank the Editor of the *Railway Magazine* and Cecil J. Allen for permission to quote details from British Locomotive Practice and Performance. We thank all photographers for their help, with a special mention of T. G. Hepburn, who has found many fine prints.

LEICESTER   *J. F. Clay*
LONDON   *J. Cliffe*
April 1972

CHAPTER ONE

The Locomotive Policy of the LNER

The period between the two great wars was the heyday of the steam locomotive. During this period the LNER was, perhaps, the most interesting railway in Britain. This is not to suggest that there was more wisdom on the LNER, nor to suggest that LNER achievements excelled those of other railways in every respect; but it is suggested that many of the happenings which appealed most to the general public took place on LNER metals.

A photograph with a high degree of contrast stands out among others and the LNER was a railway of great contrasts. It was once described as the railway which ran the best and the worst trains in the land. This referred to coaching stock. Streamliners and the East Coast expresses were running on a railway which owned more four- and six-wheeled stock than the rest of the groups put together. There were similar contrasts among the locomotives; no rival company had an express locomotive which could outrun an A4, but financial troubles had compelled the retention of large numbers of old engines for many years after their obsolescence. It was possible to travel from Leicester to Grantham in a six-wheeled coach behind an ancient Ivatt 4-4-0 in order to photograph one of the new A4s and such a trip was a great joy. The very conditions which caused dismay to the economist brought joy to the enthusiast.

At the grouping in 1923 the position of Chief Mechanical Engineer of the new group went to H. N. Gresley, the GNR chief. It has been suggested that the original intention had been to appoint J. G. Robinson from the GCR on the grounds of seniority, but this has since been the subject of some debate. It is discussed at length in *The London & North Eastern Railway* by Cecil J. Allen (Ian Allan, 1966). All forms of amalgamation cause trouble for some people who see their own chances of promotion limited and their own cherished viewpoints over-ruled by others. There were certainly men on the LNER who viewed the appointment of Gresley with dismay, but these discords remained inner conflicts which never came as near to the surface as the Midland v LNWR rivalry on the LMS. It is true that, in his monthly articles in the *Railway Magazine*, Cecil J. Allen had occasion more than once to suggest that the Gresley Pacifics were not always deployed to their best advantage on the NE section, but this was but a gentle rustle compared with the storm which raged in the same journal over the use of Midland compounds on the LMS Birmingham services.

In 1923 H. N. Gresley was just another locomotive engineer; one who had some failures and some successes. It seemed, to the outsider, that he had found the way ahead with his first two Pacifics, Nos 1470/1, but those who were intimately concerned with these engines, most especially those who wielded the shovels, knew that much modification would be needed before complete success could be claimed. Today the nature of these modifications is a matter of historical fact and it can be claimed that at the time of his death in harness in 1941 Sir Nigel Gresley held a position in public regard as high as any locomotive engineer of the 20th Century with the possible exception of G. J. Churchward of the GWR. Now that things can be seen in perspective a more realistic picture emerges and we recall the words of E. S. Cox, given as a mild rebuke to the more fanatical GWR supporters in *Chronicles of Steam* (Ian Allan, 1967): "Churchward and his successors were men not gods". It will be the aim of the writers of this book to point the same lesson to the more fanatical Gresley supporters. There will be enough solid proved success for Gresley enthusiasts not to resent this realistic approach.

The task facing Gresley in 1923 was a formidable one. He had inherited a heterogeneous collection of locomotives from a number of companies, each with its own cherished notions as to how a locomotive should be built. These had to be made into a single fleet under a single command which would operate services in a world that was becoming increasingly competitive for the railways. This all had to be done at a lower cost and with limited capital expenditure. At first Gresley continued to build engines of designs other than his own. He made no initial attempts at standardisation and showed little inclination to flood the system with GNR engines, as was the case with the LMS policy of "Midlandisation". He had no objection to building a very small class of locomotives to carry out a specific job. It is true that there were early transfers of a number of GNR Atlantics to Sheffield GC shed and of some GNR Class D1 4-4-0s to Scotland, but these were balanced by the use on the GNR of GCR four-cylinder 4-6-0s and other similar transfers. There were, of course, internal bickerings on the LNER, but on the whole changes were carried out with more tact than was the case in the early days of the

LMS. Many of the traditions of the old companies survived right up to the end of the LNER.

It was, however, soon apparent that Gresley had certain well-defined ideas as to the form that a proper locomotive should take. It will never be known how far he would have gone with a re-stocking policy had finances allowed him to do so from the very start of the LNER. As his own locomotive policy only began to reap its rewards towards the end of the inter-war period it is perhaps as well that he was restricted at first. There is no doubt about the basic principles which guided Gresley. He believed that:—

1. A large locomotive, running well within its capacity, was economical because it was master of its work.
2. The boiler should be as large as the loading gauge would allow. This was a continuation of the traditional GNR dictum that the success of a locomotive depended on its capacity to boil water.
3. Wherever possible, a three-cylinder engine with the centre valve actuated by the Gresley/Holcroft derived motion should be used.
4. The simple parallel boiler should be used where possible, though a degree of taper was introduced into the Pacific boiler through necessity. The round-top firebox was preferred to the more expensive Belpaire type.

The weakness of the Gresley locomotive in early LNER days lay in its valve design. There had been an encouraging move towards longer valve travel in the 1000 class 2-6-0 locomotives, built by the GNR in 1920. These engines had achieved great success when they handled 600 ton trains during the 1921 coal strike, averaging 50 mph over long runs and reaching maximum speeds of 75 mph. There had, however, been trouble caused by the over-running of the centre valve. With the building of the first Pacific in 1922, Gresley took the retrograde step of reverting to the old-style short-travel, short-lap valves in the vain hope that a large engine, running well within itself, would achieve economy by low combustion rates. Within a very few years this rather lame argument was destined to be shown to be a complete fallacy.

During the last few months of the North Eastern's independent existence Sir Vincent Raven had also built a three-cylinder Pacific. It has been suggested that these locomotives were hastily designed to give additional prestige to Darlington in the forthcoming grouping. In appearance the Doncaster Pacific was much more modern than the Darlington engine, which seemed to be a mere enlarged version

of the Class Z three-cylinder Atlantics. It was inevitable that the
NER Raven Pacifics and the GNR Gresley Pacifics should be
involved in comparative trials soon after the grouping and so it was
that Raven Pacific No 2400 came south on to the GNR to try
conclusions with Gresley Pacific No 1472, the engine destined later
to become the much travelled *Flying Scotsman*. The NER engine was
driven by the famous Gateshead driver T. Blades, who had fired
during the 1895 Races to Scotland, and he was well supported by
Fireman Fisher, who later became a respected locomotive inspector.
The NER engine was handled with such resolution that it reached a
standard of running never again reliably reported with this class. In
running and hp it proved to be at least the equal of the Doncaster
engine, but when the coal figures were published it was shown that
the Doncaster engine had slightly the better record with an average
figure of 3.94 lb/dbhp/hr against 4.29 lb/dbhp/hr by the NER
engine.

On the basis of these trials Gresley felt justified in proceeding with
his own design of Pacific as the standard heavy duty express engine.
In 1924 a further forty were ordered with cut down boiler mountings
which increased their range of activity. In actual fact Doncaster had
little cause for elation over the result. Although their engine had
beaten its rival by a relatively narrow margin, the figure of 3.94 lb/
dbhp/hr was not a good result on an absolute scale. In 1924 C. B.
Collett of the GWR was able to publish results of the test running of
No 4074 *Caldicot Castle*, which had achieved hp figures similar to the
LNER Pacifics but had given a coal/dbhp/hr figure of 2.83 lb. E. S.
Cox has told us how the GWR figures were not considered credible
by LMS engineers, who were used to coal figures even worse than
those of the LNER Pacifics from their large 4-6-0s. Doubtless
Doncaster engineers found similar short-term comfort in a similar
disbelief.

In October of 1923 trials were held between the various Atlantic
classes of the GNR, NER and NBR. The competing engines ran
between Newcastle and Edinburgh. The result was surprising in
that the GNR engine which had, perhaps, the highest reputation for
energetic running, was soundly beaten in coal consumption by the
NER Class Z Atlantic and by the NBR engine. If there had been any
thoughts of using the GNR engines on other sections of the East
Coast route the idea was abandoned, but a number were sent to
Sheffield GC shed. It was claimed by GCR men that the worst
engines of the class were selected for transfer, but in time the reput-

ation of the GN Atlantics at Sheffield improved and they were
responsible for some excellent work. On the GNR main line the
Atlantics continued to perform with distinction, especially on the
Pullman services, almost up to the outbreak of war.

Further test running was made in September 1924 with NER
two- and three-cylinder Atlantics and in February 1925 with two-
and three-cylinder GNR 2-8-os. The NER Atlantics ran between
Newcastle and Edinburgh and the 2-8-os ran between New England
Yard, Peterborough and Ferme Park. The conclusion was that
considerable benefits could be expected from the use of three
cylinders, but it may be questioned today whether the number of
cylinders was the real reason for the results or whether other differences such as valve design had their effect. It was, however, true that
the rival designs had similar boilers and in each case the two-
cylinder engine gave a very poor performance in terms of coal per
dbhp:

NER	Class V	2-cylinder 4-4-2	6.15 lb/dbhp/hr
NER	Class Z	3-cylinder 4-4-2	4.6 lb/dbhp/hr
GNR		2-cylinder 2-8-0	5.24 lb/dbhp/hr
GNR		3-cylinder 2-8-0	4.78 lb/dbhp/hr

None of the above figures, two-cylinder or three-cylinder, could
be considered particularly good. The GWR two-cylinder 4-6-0
"Saints" and the GWR 2800 class 2-8-os could have equalled the
running standards on no more than 3.5 lb/dbhp/hr. Nevertheless the
LNER was truly wedded to the three-cylinder engine. In support of
the test results it was stated that fifty NER Class Z three-cylinder
Atlantics had been specially observed over a year's normal running
and they showed a 13 per cent reduction in coal consumption as
compared with the twenty two-cylinder Class V Atlantics.

As capital expenditure on the LNER was limited, the bulk of the
secondary work still had to be carried on by the older classes and the
test results had shown these to be heavy on coal if the work was
related to the power output. There were a number of attempts to
reduce coal consumption by devices which had proved of value in
other countries. A number of NER Class Z Atlantics, one NBR
Atlantic, a number of GER 1500 class 4-6-os and a GNR three-
cylinder 2-8-0 were fitted with feed water heaters. Experiments with
poppet valves were carried out on some new GER Class B12 4-6-os,
some new Class D49 4-4-os, some rebuilt GCR four-cylinder 4-6-os
and on two NER Class Z Atlantics. The initial experiments had been

made on a GER Class J20 0-6-0 freight engine. The results were not sensational, although a considerable reduction in fuel consumption was claimed for the GCR 4-6-0s. It was frequently claimed that poppet-valved engines were more free running on the favourable road, but less strong on the banks than piston-valve engines. These modifications were designed to reduce coal consumption, but the American invention of the booster engine was used experimentally on a GNR Atlantic in order to assist starting ability. The full story of these trial modifications lie outside the theme of this book, but the evolution of the LNER 2-8-2 locomotives was influenced by these experiments.

The prestige of the LNER was centred very much on the Gresley Pacifics and their impressive appearance made them popular with the general public. A Pacific was proudly displayed in pristine condition at the British Empire Exhibition at Wembley in 1924, but it was with some disquiet that the LNER publicity people looked sideways at the neighbouring GWR stand where the 4-6-0 "Castle" looked so much smaller yet carried a board proclaiming it to be "Britain's Most Powerful Passenger Engine". Just what went on at managerial level is veiled in the mists of history, but the possibilities are discussed in Cecil J. Allen's *History of the LNER*. The result was that exchange trials between a GWR Castle and an LNER Pacific were arranged for late April and early May, 1925. It has been suggested that all this was done over Gresley's head and that Collett was not very pleased either. Collett, however, had nothing to fear, whereas any LNER engineer who had studied the available facts and who understood valve and front end design must have viewed the exchange with the same disquiet as an Admiralty expert on ship's armour must have viewed the prospect of the *Hood* intercepting the *Bismarck*.

As is now well known the result of the trials was that the GWR engine returned an appreciably lower coal consumption, both with its own Welsh coal on the GWR and with South Yorkshire coal on the LNER. Doncaster had some minor satisfaction during the coal strike of the following year when the Pacifics hauled 600 ton strike trains with success, while the low grade imported coal made the Castles lose all their sparkle. All the same the lessons of the 1925 exchange could not be ignored.

In 1924 plans had been prepared for an improved valve gear for the Gresley Pacifics, but Gresley appeared reluctant to authorise any change. The new gear would have introduced long-lap and long-travel valves and with this gear the results of the 1925 exchanges could have been far different. The shelving of this excellent notion was said to be because the performance of the Gresley Pacifics was "already satisfactory", but this opinion was not the result of a unanimous vote among the firemen. The humiliation at the hands of the smaller GWR machine and the resultant publicity was most unwelcome to the LNER and it cast a damper on the celebrations of Centenary Year.

It was characteristic of Gresley that he was slow to move from a position once adopted. It has also been suggested that his subordinates were reluctant to tell him unwelcome news. At first a minimum alteration was made to the valve motion of engine No 4477 and the good results which followed led to engine No 2555 being given the full treatment with long-lap, long-travel gear as envisaged in 1924. Coal consumption took a sensational dive from the former average of 55 lb/mile to 38 lb/mile on the same duties and the engine proved to be a more lively runner. It is said that even then Gresley was reluctant to move and not until he had himself observed the running of 2555 from the footplate was he convinced and ordered the conversion of all the Pacifics to conform with 2555. It is to the credit of Gresley that, once the decision was made, there was no turning back and further experiments were made by fitting 220 lb boilers and larger superheaters to engines Nos 4480 and 2544. Test running in 1928 with engine No 4473 with original boiler of 180 lb pressure but with the improved gear and with No 2544 with the 220 lb boiler gave results of 3.08 lb/dbhp/hr for 4473 and 3.12 lb/dbhp/hr for 2544. If the calorific correction for the quality of coal is made, then the LNER had now attained the same thermal efficiency as the GWR.

In 1929 the first Paris Orleans Pacific, rebuilt by Chapelon became the most efficient steam locomotive the world had seen up till then and in 1932 the rebuilding of another class as a 4-8-0 proved to the world that even more sensational performance was possible. Gresley was a great admirer of Chapelon but, apart from his experimental high-pressure locomotive No 10000, he shrank from compounding which, in any case, would have been difficult to exploit within our restricted loading gauge. He was, however, impressed by details of Chapelon's work and carried out further experiments with feed water heaters on two Pacifics Nos 2576 and 2580. The Chapelon influence was destined to influence future LNER policy.

Such, then, was the world into which the LNER 2-8-2s and 2-6-2s were introduced. It was a world of large boilers, three cylinders and no reluctance to try foreign devices which could improve efficiency. From 1927 onwards LNER policy was fully wedded to long-lap, long-travel valves. Fully to appreciate how the LNER 2-8-2s and 2-6-2s fitted into the general LNER pattern of progress needs a chronological table of the significant events:

1922   First Gresley Pacific.
1923   Grouping of British railways.
1923   Gresley appointed CME of LNER.
1923   Experimental booster fitted to Atlantic No 4419.
1925   Exchange with GWR "Castle".
1925   First Class P1 2-8-2 freight engine built.
1927   Improved valve motion on No 2555.
1927   220 lb boilers on Nos 4480 and 2544.
1929   First Chapelon rebuilt Pacific.
1932   First Chapelon rebuilt 4-8-0.
1934   First Class P2 2-8-2 built.
1936   First Class V2 2-6-2 built.
1941   Death of Sir Nigel Gresley.
1941   E. Thompson appointed CME of LNER.
1941   Further V4 construction cancelled.
1942   First Class B1 4-6-0, two-cylinder policy adopted for smaller engines.
1943   First P2 2-8-2 converted to a 4-6-2.

CHAPTER TWO

The History of the 2-8-2 Type

Large numbers of 2-8-2 type engines were built for various railways the world over. A total of over 14000 were built in the US alone. In America it was mainly intended for freight service, but in Europe a number of classes were used on express duties, mainly over heavy grades and on mixed traffic work. The advantages of the type for heavy work were considerable and Gresley was fully justified in giving the type a trial. The boilers could be interchangeable with a Pacific type express locomotive, the trailing truck permitted the use of a large wide fire-box without any undue raising of the centre of gravity. Providing that speeds were not intended to be unduly high the type gave good riding stability especially if, as in American practice, the leading and trailing carrying wheels were equalised with the adjacent driving wheels. It was not always the practice in Europe to have equalising beams in the American manner. A disadvantage of the type was that some sacrifice of adhesion weight had to be accepted as compared with a 2-10-0 of similar size, but the 2-8-2 usually allowed slightly larger driving wheels than a 2-8-0 or 2-10-0. The 2-8-2 was thus inferior to a Pacific for speed and inferior to a 2-10-0 for slow heavy freight haulage, but it was superior to either for mixed traffic duties. This of course assumes similar boiler and cylinder efficiency.

The spiritual home of the type was the United States and one of the earliest examples to be built emerged in 1897 from the Baldwin Locomotive Works for the 3 ft 6 in gauge Japanese Government Railways. This gave the type the name "Mikado" class. This name remained in general use in Britain and America, but during World War 2 any connection with Japan caused revulsion and attempts were made to change the name to the "MacArthur" class. At first the new name was accepted with enthusiasm, but as the war receded into history the old name gradually crept back into favour. The first large heavy 2-8-2 class built in quantity for heavy main line service in the US was introduced in 1905 when the American Locomotive Company built a number of engines for the Northern Pacific Railway. This railroad had been operating the easy grades with

2-6-2 type engines and the heavy grades with 2-8-0s, but the latter could not manage the same loads. The 2-8-2s climbed the grades with the loads the 2-6-2s managed on the level.

These Northern Pacific engines set the future standard for the 2-8-2 for heavy freight service in America. They were true examples of the type with a wide firebox having a grate area of 43.5 sq ft, driving wheels 5 ft 3 in in diameter and a boiler pressure of 200 lb/sq in. In those saturated days they must have extended firemen to their physical limit, but they handled the desired tonnage while other engines were exhausting their firemen and failing to do that. Modifications were suggested by experience and these included combustion chambers. As time passed and superheaters and mechanical stokers allowed larger and more powerful examples to be built many American roads adopted the type and in some cases 2-8-0 engines were converted to 2-8-2.

An interesting example was built for the Pennsylvania RR in 1918. This engine had a boiler interchangeable with the famous K4S Pacific and it is of particular interest in that full details of its test performance on the Altoona Plant are available. The engine produced 2800 ihp at 29 mph, but this required an evaporation rate of 58000 lb/hr and a coal consumption of 4.2 lb/ihp/hr. This was one of the heaviest specific coal consumption figures published for a Pennsylvania RR engine, but a reduction to 2000 ihp brought the consumption rate down to a reasonable 2.7 lb/ihp/hr. At the highest rate of evaporation blast pipe pressure was 16 lb/sq in, while at the more moderate power output blast pipe pressure was 5.5 lb. American freight engines of fifty years ago must have made a rare racket on the banks.

The position of the 2-8-2 type in American locomotive stock is indicated by the situation when the American Railroads came under Government control during World War I. A Locomotive Committee was formed from the three chief firms building locomotives and they approved twelve standard designs, which became known as the USRA engines. The designs were, however, not ready until 1919, by which time war was happily over. In 1920 the railroads resumed private ownership and the standardisation programme was abandoned. By then 1830 standard engines had been built and the two 2-8-2 classes accounted for almost half the total. The two classes proposed were based on fireboxes of 66.7 sq ft and 70.8 sq ft. Driving wheels were 5 ft 3 in, which seems to have been the favourite size for 2-8-2 wheels in the US. There were some conversions to 5 ft 10 in, but such a wheel size never became popular for American 2-8-2s.

The maximum development of the 2-8-2 type came in 1924 with a class built for the Delaware, Lackawanna & Western. These engines were based on the larger USRA machines with a 70.4 sq ft grate but a tractive effort of 67000 lb, increased 11500 lb by the booster. Booster equipment began to be popular in the US between the wars. In the following year the LIMA Company built for the New York Central an experimental 2-8-4 which was in effect the basic American 2-8-2 with a larger firebox of 100 sq ft.

The 2-8-4 type from then onwards tended to eclipse the 2-8-2 for the heaviest duties. The larger boiler did nothing to increase starting power, but it did allow for the development of more dbhp at speed. The 2-8-2 type in the US did some passenger service on secondary lines and on heavy gradients, but it did not loom very large in express running. When the final tally of the American steam locomotive was made it emerged that the 2-8-2 was the most numerous wheel arrangement, with over 14000 as the total, which included 9500 for heavy main line service.

In selecting the 2-8-2 type for his experimental freight locomotives of 1925 Gresley was following a tradition well established in America. It is suggested by F. S. Brown in his book *Nigel Gresley Locomotive Engineer* (Ian Allan, 1961) that the Pennsylvania K4S influenced the design of the Gresley Pacific and that it was a logical conclusion to assume that the 1925 LNER freight Mikados followed the precedent of the Pennsylvania 2-8-2, which had the same boiler as the K4S Pacific. It was, however, in European practice that Gresley found the inspiration for his 2-8-2 express engines.

The fastest running 2-8-2 locomotives were to be found in Germany. In 1918 the Saxon State Railway introduced a large 2-8-2 express engine known as the Saxon XX HV class. This engine was intended for use on the mountainous routes between Bavaria, Saxony and Silesia. It was a four-cylinder compound with 6 ft 3 in driving wheels. The leading axle and the leading pair of coupled wheels were combined in a Krauss-Helmholtz truck, giving the engine a decided advantage on sharply curved track as compared with a 2-8-2 with conventional suspension. Shortly before the amalgamation into the Deutsche Reichsbahn, the Prussian State Railway put into service the P 10 class 2-8-2, generally similar but with three-cylinder simple propulsion and smaller driving wheels of 5 ft 9 in. These engines were officially classified as passenger locomotives and they were employed almost exclusively on express service on hilly sections throughout Germany. At the time of its construction this class was considered to be the most powerful passenger class in Germany. When the late R. E. Charlewood timed one of these engines on the densely occupied high-speed section between Leipzig and Berlin, No 39.103 hauled a 415 ton train over the 102.2 miles in 109 min 36 sec. The engines were clearly capable of fast running.

Some four-cylinder compound 2-8-2 express engines were built in 1922 in Italy. These had driving wheels of 6 ft 2 in in diameter and were four-cylinder compounds. In 1926 ten of them were fitted with Caprotti gear. These engines had a low axle loading and a resulting wide range of activity, but they were languid performers on the road. The Italian flair for designing very fast motor cars does not seem to have been applied to steam locomotives, but they showed considerable talent for building fast electric trains. There were many more 2-8-2 locomotive classes in Europe, but they were mainly used for freight and mixed traffic duties. There was no reason, however, for Gresley to reject the 2-8-2 as a fast-running locomotive; the German locomotives alone had a record good enough to justify the choice.

It might very easily have been that Gresley was the one to build the second 2-8-2 type engine in Britain. In *Locomotive Panorama* Vol 1 (Ian Allan, 1965), E. S. Cox has described how between 1923 and the retirement of G. Hughes in 1925 work was proceeding on the design of a four-cylinder Pacific and a corresponding 2-8-2 with the same boiler. The building of the first Gresley Pacific in 1922 had acted as a spur to those who favoured Hughes' big engine policy for the LMS, but they were opposed by an operating department under Midland influence which wanted small engines. Had the big engine school won the day the LMS might have anticipated the Gresley 2-8-2, though not of course the Pacific which had been built by the GNR in 1922 before the grouping. The need for a powerful freight engine was greater on the LMS than on the LNER. By the end of 1924 the original four-cylinder simple proposal for the 2-8-2 had changed to a three-cylinder project and the delay meant that little real progress had been made by the time Hughes retired, to be replaced by Fowler. Despite the rule now being entirely Midland the development work continued, now with a rival Garratt proposal as the 2-8-2 was giving anxiety over axle loading on the Toton-Brent section, which was to be its chief sphere of activity. Thus it was that the LNER 2-8-2 was running while the LMS design was still in a relatively early stage of development. After the LNER engine was built the LMS Garratt project was carried through to fulfilment while the 2-8-2 had been re-schemed as a four-cylinder compound and finally abandoned.

It was as a junior engineer that E. S. Cox, who has told the story of the LMS design offices so graphically in his various Ian Allan books, was involved in the early LMS 2-8-2 project. But it was in a senior capacity as locomotive officer in charge of design that he was concerned in a later 2-8-2 design in the BR standard range. It is told in *British Standard Steam Railway Locomotives* (Ian Allan, 1966) how this design was rejected in favour of a 2-10-0.

It has not been the aim in this chapter to catalogue all the 2-8-2 engines the world has ever seen—such a project would demand a bigger book than this—but it is hoped to indicate some of the aspects of 2-8-2 history that have a significant bearing on the Gresley engines. It will be seen that the record of the 2-8-2 in other countries fully justifies its choice. In post-war days, after the Gresley engines had been scrapped, there appeared two classes which probably had the most distinguished record of all the 2-8-2s.

Early in 1945 a large order was given by the SNCF for 2-8-2 mixed traffic engines from the three main locomotive builders of the United States. Some locomotives were lost at sea, but finally 1323 engines of Class 141R entered service in France. These simple two-cylinder engines had a lower thermal efficiency on test than the corresponding French design, the 141P, a four-cylinder compound developed from a former PLM engine but with Chapelon features. In this form the 141P matched the efficiency figures of the Chapelon 4-8-0s and so shared the honour of being the world's most efficient steam locomotive. This was based on its proved efficiency as a heat engine as measured on the test plant, but there are many shrewd observers who think that if full commercial efficiency was taken into account, including availability, mileage and maintenance costs, then the Amercan built 141R was the engine that showed the lowest annual, costs per ton of load hauled, of any engine in France.

Such then was the record of the 2-8-2 class in world history. It is a distinguished record. A 2-8-2 is claimed, on the basis of valid test figures, to be the world's most efficient steam locomotive. The 2-8-2 became the most numerous type to be built in the United States. There must have been some virtue and it is interesting to find how the LNER examples performed against such a background.

CHAPTER THREE

The P1 Mikados

In the summer of 1925 one of the writers of this book, then aged eleven, was watching the traffic on the former GNR main line at the road bridge just to the south of Peascliffe Tunnel. To his surprise there emerged from the tunnel a type of engine he had never seen before. Running light and obviously quite new it made its way southwards. Mentioning this engine later in adult company the boy described it as being "Like a black Pacific with small wheels" and he was told that it was only to be expected that Doncaster would build a large goods engine to match their large passenger Pacifics. This non-technical explanation perhaps got as near to the truth behind the design as anything that has appeared since from sources more expert. The exact reason for the building of the two freight 2-8-2s remains something of a mystery. There was certainly no pressing need for a freight engine of this size and power on the LNER and it would be true to say that there was more need for such an engine on the LMS to deal with the Toton-Brent mineral traffic.

It may have been that Gresley was following the precedent of the Pennsylvania RR, who followed their K4 Pacific design by a 2-8-2 freight engine with the same boiler. It is generally supposed that Gresley had been influenced by the K4 design when he introduced his Pacific. Against this theory it can be said that Gresley can hardly have studied the design of the K4 in detail or he would have adopted the large, long-travel valves which were the secret of the success of the K4 and the E6 Atlantic as compared with earlier US engines. It has also been suggested that the LNER 2-8-2 engines were built as an operational experiment to test the practical problem of operating very long coal trains rather than as an exercise in locomotive design.

There had been considerable interest in super freight engines just before World War I. An outline drawing survives of a huge 2-10-0 freight engine designed at Horwich for the L & Y following the visit of a number of officials to Belgium in 1912. They had returned full of enthusiasm for the Flamme 2-10-0s and it is doubtful if the enthusiasm of the fact-finding delegation to Belgium would have been shared by enginemen had the idea been carried to completion. A line drawing of the proposed engine appears in *Chronicles of Steam* by E. S. Cox (Ian Allan, 1967). At about the same time J. G. Robinson was thinking in terms of some even larger engines for the coal traffic which it was hoped to move between the South Yorkshire coalfields and the newly opened port of Immingham. This was indeed a bold proposal which would have involved some civil engineering work to relax loading gauge restrictions over this specific route. Robinson was thinking in terms of 100 wagon trains of 40 ton bogie wagons and these were to have been hauled by some monster 2-10-2 freight locomotives. One design came from the Baldwin Locomotive Works, USA and the other from Gorton resembled a monstrously overgrown GCR "Tiny" 2-8-0. Line drawings of these engines can be studied in *The Great Central*, Vol 3 by George Dow (Ian Allan, 1965). Both the GCR and the L & Y projects were many years ahead of their time and they hardly emerge as practical commercial propositions.

After the war there was resurgence of interest in large freight engines as money came less easily to railway companies and all means of seeking more economical working had to be sought. There was a strong desire to move freight in longer trains. The L & Y rethought the idea of a large engine in articulated form. The first idea was a 2-6-0-0-6-2 Garratt, which changed into a 2-6-2-2-6-2 and which started the chain of events destined finally to materialise in the LMS Garratts of 1927. There was an alternative Horwich 0-6-6-0 Mallet and the Midland had considered a similar engine as an alternative to the 0-10-0 Lickey banker. Drawings of the L & Y proposals can be seen in books by E. S. Cox and the Midland engine in *Derby Works and Midland Locomotives* by J. B. Radford (Ian Allan, 1971). Although the 0-10-0 was intended as a banking engine the Midland was sufficiently interested in a large main line freight engine to try the Lickey banker on the Toton-Brent service, but it was an abject failure.

In the early days of the grouping Hughes had been working on the design of a four-cylinder Pacific and a corresponding 2-8-2. Before his retirement these had changed to three-cylinder projects, only to be changed again to four-cylinder compound engines in Fowler's time. Had it not been for these vacillations the LMS might have been first to introduce a large freight engine, but as things turned out it was not until 1927 that the first LMS Garratt appeared and by then the large Gresley engines had been running for two years. Gresley was doubtless aware that something was developing in the LMS drawing offices. He was especially happy to be the first in the field with his 2-8-2 and to make the new engine one of the showpieces at the Darlington Centenary celebrations in 1925.

The first LNER 2-8-2 was actually built in July 1925 and it made a most impressive show alongside the even larger 2-8-8-2 Garratt at the Centenary. It was a declaration of the LNER's intention to take a leading position in British locomotive practice. Had it not been for nasty lingering doubts following the exchange running against the GWR "Castle", Doncaster's joy would have been unconfined.

The most striking departure from normal practice in Britain was the booster, which increased the engine's tractive effort and adhesion weight at starting. The booster was of the Franklin type and some experimental work had been done on Atlantic No 4419. The booster was at that time making considerable headway in the US and the 4-6-4 express engine and the 2-8-4 freight engine owed much of their success to its application. On the LNER engine the booster increased tractive effort from 38500 lb to 47000 lb; this was intended to be used when starting and when topping the 1 in 200 banks. It was intended to make the haulage of 1600 ton coal trains an everyday all-weather possibility and to work 2000 tons in special test conditions. The clutch cylinder for engaging the booster was operated by air from Westinghouse type pump on the side of the boiler.

The engine had ample boiler power to haul the immense trains that could be started with the aid of a booster. The boiler was the same as that used on the Pacifics and of course in 1925 was pressed at 180 lb/sq in. The booster was, a drain on the boiler, but it would never need to be cut in for long enough to exhaust the steam supply irrevocably. The driving wheels were 5 ft 2 in in diameter, which was larger than the normal 4 ft 8 in of contemporary 2-8-0s. It may have been that Gresley welcomed the larger wheels in anticipation of the time when all freight moved faster, but the main reason was fitting the length of the engine to the Pacific boiler. In the event the engines spent almost their whole life on slow loose-coupled trains. The cylinders were of the same type as used on the Pacifics, with the same 20 in diameter and 26 in stroke. They had the same short lap, $1\frac{1}{4}$ in, but cut off in full gear was increased to 75 per cent as compared with 65 per cent in the case of the Pacifics. This meant an increase in valve travel from $4\frac{9}{16}$ in the Pacifics to $5\frac{1}{2}$ in on the 2-8-2s. The increase to 75 per cent was made to improve starting and lessen the risk of the engine stopping in the "blind" position, as sometimes happened with the Pacifics.

A special six-wheeled tender was designed for the 2-8-2s with space for the location of the non-standard locomotive dragbox, which incorporated the booster pipes. When the P1s were scrapped these tenders needed modification before they could be used on Thompson 4-6-0s. At first the tenders had the letters LNER with the number below, but later the number was moved to the cab side and the letters LNER were moved to a more central position on the tender. They were painted in the LNER goods engine black and in wartime the letters were reduced to NE only.

The pioneer engine No 2393 was allocated to New England depot after its appearance at the Darlington celebrations and in November 1925 it was joined by No 2394. This engine was fitted with a larger "E" type superheater with 62 elements as against the 32 element superheater on No 2393. The large superheater had the impressive heating surface of 1104 sq ft, but no discernable advantage accrued and only about 30 deg F extra superheat was obtained. The extra degrees were in fact less than the fluctuation which took place during a run. The boilers suffered from frequent cinder blockage in the flue tubes since these were only $3\frac{1}{2}$ in in diameter due to the single element feature of the "E" type design. Protagonists of the "E" type superheater claimed that the LNER application was incorrect and that success could hardly have been expected. In the US the "E" type boilers had larger flue tubes and the whole boiler consisted of flues only without firetubes. It may equally well be argued that there was little to be gained by pushing the degree of superheat up far above that needed to combat condensation in the cylinders through the range of normal working conditions. A similar 62-element super-heater was used for experimental trials on Pacific No 2562 and again the results were disappointing. The boilers which had the large superheaters could always be identified by the presence of two air snifting valves behind the chimney.

In service the P1s could handle coal trains of 100 loaded wagons, but from the operational viewpoint such trains were a hazard. They were too long for many of the sidings on the route and they occupied track circuits which slowed down following trains. The enginemen and guards complained that they had difficulty in carrying out working rules and regulations since the two ends of the train were out of sight of each other at certain points. The engines were not loved by the enginemen nor by the operating people. They were reputed to be very heavy coal burners and the initial dynamometer car trials were never followed by published results, but those who saw the figures described them as "disappointing". One figure that has come to light was in a "Locomotive Inspectors' Conference Report" presented to a meeting at Liverpool Street in 1926. This reads "Locos Nos 2393 and 2394 coal consumption 131 lb per mile" and this was endorsed "What can we do with these engines?" The inspectors were asked for their comments.

A coal/mile figure of 131 lb may cause hands to be raised in pious horror but the figure must be related to the size of the engine, the loads hauled and to the contemporary coal figures of engines of similar size and power. It may also be that during 1926 coal of a lower than normal quality may have affected the results. The high figure is, however, in keeping with the general reputation. We are fortunate in that the LMS Garratts, which were hauling comparable loads, are very fully documented in the various Ian Allan books written by E. S. Cox. These LMS tests with loads varying from 1185 to 1556 tons were over a rather harder road than New England to Ferme Park. The coal per mile figures for the Garratts varied between 97 and 144 lb per mile and coal/dbhp/hr figures from 3.61 to 3.86. Now if the LNER 2-8-2s were hauling loads of up to 1600 tons the figure of 131 lb/mile as an all-weather average as compared with test conditions was not greatly different, having regard to the more difficult Midland road. The LMS test trains ran via Melton.

We can form a rough estimate of the coal/dbhp/hr figure to be expected of a P1 from the contemporary results of the Gresley Pacifics in their original form with short lap gear. No 1472 on test in 1923 returned a coal/dbhp/hr figure of 3.94 lb when engaged on express service between Doncaster and Kings Cross. It is well known that more favourable coal/dbhp/hr figures are obtained on slow freight services than on expresses for the simple reason that more of the engine's total power is available at the drawbar at slow speeds. It would be reasonable to expect that the LNER 2-8-2s would return a coal/dbhp/hr figure very similar to that of the LMS Garratts. Both designs suffered from having the old style short-lap, short-travel valves. The coal consumption of the LNER engines may be considered as being heavy on an absolute scale, but no more than average by contemporary standards. More favourable coal/dbhp/hr figures were obtained by the freight engines of the 2-8-0 and 2-10-0 types during the 1948 Exchanges.

In practice the boosters gave a lot of trouble; the cabs were usually filled with steam when they were in use and the additional steam consumption added to the fireman's burden. Normally the booster was only used at starting and it would perhaps be cut in for a mile or two towards the summit of a 1 in 200 bank. It was useful when a full load had to be started at Cambridge Junction, Hitchin, and taken up to Stevenage Summit. Further trouble was caused by the fracturing of the booster steam pipe connections. This trouble was made worse by the sharp curves of the New England triangle. The engines were frequently stopped in the shed awaiting spare parts for the booster. When the boosters were removed in the mid 1930s no one was sorry.

The boosters were really only needed when maximum loads were worked and this only happened when the engines were relatively new. It was found that for convenient operation loads had to be reduced to 92 wagons and as time went on this load in practice declined to something nearer to the 80 wagons worked by the 2-8-0s.

From 1932 onwards the practice of working shorter but faster coal trains hauled by Class K3 2-6-0s was found to give good results. These trains consisted of 56 wagons with a 50 ton bogie brick wagon with vacuum brake between the engine and train for additional braking power. As acceleration of passenger trains continued after 1932 the need to reduce line occupation by long heavy freight trains became more urgent. The coal trade continued to be depressed and it followed that the 2-8-2s had been a less than successful operational experiment.

Other more dramatic locomotive adventures took place on the LNER in the mid-1930s and no one had much interest in the P1s. They were driven by a special link at New England shed and it is said that drivers from outside the link were scared of handling them. It is likely that few had any ambition to try. During the initial planning stage of *Cock o' the North* No 2394 was tried on the 7.45 am semi-fast from King's Cross and speeds of up to 65 mph were attained. The fireman is said to have been thankful not to have been going beyond Peterborough.

The Second World War brought reduced standards of locomotive maintenance and this was a disaster for the P1s. In 1942 they were both fitted with A3-type 220 lb boilers and their cylinders were reduced to the 19 in diameter of the A3s. This raised the tractive effort to 42500 lb. No confirmation can be found for the suggestion that they had long lap valves fitted at the same time and the LNER diagram of 1942 shows short lap valves. Whatever is the truth about the valves it is an established fact that any alterations did nothing to increase the popularity of the class. The rebuilding with A3 boilers lifted the P1s from Power class 8 to 9. They had a wide route availability, RA 7, but in practice stayed on their own route. The only occasion that one was seen north of Peterborough by one of the writers, apart from an initial sighting in 1925, was at Grantham in 1943.

A former locomotive inspector recalls one of the engines standing in Grantham locomotive yard in 1925 and being given a most critical appraisal by enginemen. The men were not enthusiastic and they saw in the multiplication of giant locomotives harder work and slower promotion. An opinion was expressed that "She's an ugly brute" but the late O. V. S. Bulleid, who had a very high regard for the class, said that they were the most handsome engines Gresley ever built. This merely confirms that the appearance of a locomotive varies with the viewpoint. Some of their workings from New England were at night but it was always a point of interest when travelling south on a GN line express to keep an eye open in the hope of seeing one of the Mikados plodding its way southwards on the slow road.

When the war was over and the volume of heavy freight declined Thompson scrapped both engines in 1945, their still serviceable boilers being transferred to Pacifics. They had gained the doubtful honour of being the first Gresley engines to be scrapped by intention. An A4 had been scrapped after being damaged by enemy bombs at York. In general the P1s can hardly be called successful engines, but part of their failure can be ascribed to lack of suitable work. Had their introduction coincided with the more general use of high-capacity wagons they might have found more useful employment. There were details of their design which proved to be of doubtful value and the boosters were of more trouble than they were worth. The idea of a booster was, however, an excellent one which might have been of great help to the Pacifics, especially in Scotland and in starting exceptionally heavy trains from King's Cross. The booster allowed for the successful multiplication of the 4-6-4 and 2-8-4 types in the US but they were quite pleased to manage without it as the 4-8-4s were developed. The introduction of a large freight engine for general service had to wait for the Riddles 2-10-0 in 1954. The New England examples of the standard 9F class undertook mixed traffic duties far faster than anything expected of a P1 even on its one assay in passenger haulage. Perhaps the general conception of the 1925 Gresley 2-8-2 was not fundamentally unsound but it was certainly ahead of its time.

CHAPTER FOUR

Cock o' the North

The advent of No 2001 *Cock o' the North* was a landmark in British express locomotive history. Nothing like it was seen in this country before or since. On paper, at least, it was the most powerful express locomotive ever built for a British railway as it held the leading position both in tractive effort and in boiler size. Gresley had been much impressed by the remarkable results obtained by Chapelon on the Paris Orleans Railway with his rebuilt compound locomotives. Gresley had maintained close contact with Chapelon and he decided to build, for use on the Edinburgh–Aberdeen road, an engine in which traditional LNER features were wedded to some of the best ideas from France. The Chapelon features were enlarged, streamlined, steam passages and ports, the Kylchap double blastpipe and the ACFI feed-water heater, but these devices were applied to a three-cylinder simple engine instead of a four-cylinder compound. Chapelon had used the 4-8-0 wheel arrangement for engines intended for heavy grade work such as was to be faced on the NBR main line, but Gresley preferred the 2-8-2 type as this permitted the location of a wide firebox while the trailing wheels under the cab improved the riding qualities of the engine. Gains at the rear end, however, meant that a price was to be paid at the front. Doubts were expressed later about the value of the two-wheeled leading truck in guiding the engine round sharp curves. It was suggested that the leading pair of coupled wheels had to take an undue share of the stresses and overheating resulted. The position could have been made better had it been possible to use the Krauss Helmholtz or the Zara leading truck, but the position of the inside cylinder prevented this, while the outside slide bars precluded the use of spring controlled side play in the leading coupled axle.

The boiler was a straightforward enlargement of the A3 Pacific boiler with the same barrel, but with the firebox lengthened by 15 in to give 50 sq ft of grate area. In practice this 50 sq ft grate did not prove to be completely successful. The engines were never popular with the man who had to do the work. The fireman's problem was keeping the very large grate covered with a thick enough layer of coal to avoid air blowing through and cooling the fire. It can be argued that 50 sq ft grates were just too large for hand firing and perhaps a 45 sq ft grate would have given equal or better results. It was only in special test conditions that engines with these very large grates achieved outputs commensurate with their grate areas. The advantage that can be claimed for the larger grate was that it allowed lower combustion rates per sq ft of grate area at existing firing rates. It was claimed that the larger grates were an advantage with the lower grades of coal, but frequently it only resulted in wasteful covering of unused firebars. The Peppercorn A1 Pacifics had the reputation of burning more coal than Pacifics with smaller grates when used on the relatively easy jobs that were most prevalent on the main lines in the 1950s.

The mating of the A3 boiler barrel with the 50 sq ft grate altered the boiler proportions, with the result that the free area through the tubes was reduced to 12.4 per cent against the 15 per cent of the Pacifics and the V2s. This low percentage did not comply with the minimum values established in the paper given by Loubster and Cox in 1938, but the necessity is arguable; it is possible to cite examples of engines with a good reputation for steaming with free gas areas no higher. In all cases, however, the low gas area was associated with a very strong blast if favourable steaming results were obtained and in the case of *Cock o' the North* high smokebox vacuum with minimum back pressure was sought by the use of the Kylchap double blastpipe. This device had been used with great success on the Chapelon compounds in France, but some of the earlier applications in Britain, not only on the P2s but on the Southern "Lord Nelson" and the LMS "Jubilee", suggest that the ideal proportions for a simple engine had not then been finalised.

As built No 2001 was fitted with Lentz rotary cam poppet valve gear arranged to give infinitely variable cut-off. The valves were mounted horizontally and there were four valves per cylinder. The inlet valves were 8 in in diameter and the exhaust valves 9 in. The two large diameter valves were mounted side by side at each end of the cylinder and the valves were driven by twin camshafts driven by propeller shafts from the second pair of driving wheels on each side of the engine. Each camshaft operated six valves, including two from the inside cylinder. The valve layout resulted in large clearance volumes, which were over 12 per cent for the outside cylinders and 16 per cent for the inside. An excessive amount of lead advance steam had to be provided in the valve timing. None of these features was conducive to high cylinder efficiency unless abnormally early cut-offs and low power outputs were accepted. Another disadvantage was the sudden opening of the exhaust which the poppet valves allowed, causing sharp peaks in the exhaust beat which had a tendency to tear the fire and cause fire throwing. The separate valve events were attractive in as far as they gave a fuller toe to the indicator diagram, but the adverse effect on the draughting was a heavy price to pay for a small increase in power.

These adverse effects became apparent when No 2001 was tested on the open road in France. It became virtually impossible to fire the locomotive to maintain high power outputs. A complete solution of the problem was not possible and the shortcomings of a number of classes of poppet-valve engines remain shrouded in mystery. It would seem that the engine reached its grate limit at a modest steaming rate and increased firing only resulted in more unburnt fuel going up the chimney. A similar situation seems to have afflicted the BR Pacific No 71000, also fitted with poppet valves. The later P2s with piston valves were lighter on coal, but they still suffered from fire throwing when working heavily at low speeds. It may have been that the Kylchap exhaust was regarded with suspicion at Doncaster, quite unjustly, and as a result of this the A4s reverted to single blast with a Churchward jumper top. It is possible now, with hindsight, to regret this, for the subsequent record of the Kylchap exhaust, properly proportioned on the A4s, suggests that the "Coronation" might have been handled with greater ease by a larger stud of double blastpipe A4s at King's Cross and Haymarket.

Grate losses and poor combustion might have stemmed from a number of other causes. It may have been that there was insufficient firebox volume in relation to the grate area. This would prevent there being space for the complete burning of every particle of fuel. *Cock o' the North* actually had a firebox volume ratio on the low side in comparison with the boilers later produced by Doncaster for the A4 and the V2. Large air spaces through the bars of the grate of an engine with strong blast can allow too much air to be drawn through the bed to tear and cool the fire. Unburnt fuel can also drop down into the ashpan. It is possible that *Cock o' the North* could have benefited from a closer spacing of fire bars. Bulleid suggested that modifications to the ashpan could have been of benefit but Gresley ignored this. This criticism may have been justified if ash accumulation was causing air restriction in the lengthened rear and side portion of the grate. It appears that Doncaster recognised that some changes in boiler proportions could have been of some use as the last engine, No 2006, had an enlarged firebox with a combustion chamber and a barrel shortened by one foot.

One can conjecture that comparatively small alterations might have improved the P2s, but the fact has to be faced that the boiler definitely appeared to present difficulties in maximum steaming conditions. This being said, *Cock o' the North* was a magnificent example of locomotive engineering. Doncaster works were justifiably proud of its first-class workmanship and construction, which drew appreciative comment from French engineers during its visit to Vitry. In particular the monobloc casting with the three 21 in cylinders and the twelve valve ports was a fine piece of foundry work for which the late R. A. Thom, the former Tuxford Locomotive Superintendent of the LD & EC, was partly responsible. The Doncaster boiler shop was also very proud of its work in those days. The difficult job of staying the round top firebox was achieved by the perfect matching of the holes between inner and outer wrappers. Certainly Doncaster seemed to suffer less from staybolt troubles than certain other lines in those days.

The ACFI feed water heater was used on the new engine. The LNER had experimented with such devices on a number of former NER C7 Atlantics and on some former GER B12 4-6-0s. It was hoped that this would take the place of an exhaust steam injector, but in practice the savings over the conventional Davies and Metcalfe pattern exhaust injector did not justify its further use. Subsequent engines of the class were equipped with the conventional injectors similar to the Pacifics and No 2001 was altered to conform. A chime whistle added distinction to the new engine and this feature later became more famous still on the A4s. The wedge-shaped cab front recalled the wind cutter cabs of the French PLM and the angled glasses reduced glare at night.

Cock o' the North had an eight-wheeled tender which resembled those used on the final batch of A3s, but actually it was something of an experiment. It was of the high-sided, non-corridor type, but it had spoked instead of disc wheels and the body was of all-welded construction. These modifications reduced the weight by $2\frac{1}{2}$ tons, but later examples returned to the disc wheels. The original tender remained with *Cock o' the North* throughout. The tender was large enough to appear suitable for the engine and the criticism that was directed against the first LMS Pacific was not directed against the new LNER engine. The distinctive sloping smokebox and semi-streamlining was not received with the same enthusiasm in this country, but it was later copied by Cockerill of the Belgian National Railways for his new four-cylinder Pacifics. There is little doubt that 2001 had created quite an impression on the Continent.

The second engine of the class, No 2002 *Earl Marischal*, appeared in the autumn of 1934. This engine had 9 in piston valves and the clearance volume was reduced to 7.5 per cent with normal lead values. The soft blast of this engine caused drifting of steam over the cab windows and a second outer pair of smoke deflector plates had to be fitted. The second engine must have been considered the better machine, as the further batch of P2s were basically similar, but the A4-type streamlined nose was grafted on to the front in place of the original type of smokebox and deflectors. There were a few detailed modifications within the class. No 2005 was built with a single Kylala blast pipe instead of the double Kylchap type. The greater diameter of the chimney made the outer casing wider than that of a single blast A4 and the difference between No 2005 and other engines of the later batch of P2s is only apparent from photographs taken at certain angles.

The final example, No 2006, had the combustion chamber at the front of the firebox; this was classified as type 108 instead of boiler type 106 on the earlier engines. No 2004 was given an experimental fitting with the aim of reducing the heavy pull on the firebed when the engine was working hard. A bypass pipe was fitted to the base of the blastpipe exhausting to the atmosphere behind the chimney. The idea was to siphon off some of the exhaust steam when the engine was working hard and so to reduce the smoke box vacuum to more normal values. Several adjustments were made to this, but in practice only a marginal reduction of vacuum took place. The plug valve operating the bypass pipe suffered from carbonisation and trouble eventually spread to the pipe itself which became difficult to maintain. The device was removed after a few years.

Cock o' the North was a marriage of much that was best in British and French practice. The engines might have achieved greater success had they not been intended for the tortuous Edinburgh–Aberdeen road. It had been hoped that the rigid wheelbase of 19 ft 6 in and thinned tyres on the two centre pairs of wheels would have allowed the engines to traverse the curves without difficulty. In practice this hope proved to have been unduly optimistic and the engines were beset with mechanical troubles.

A weakness of the design was that too many pieces of standard practice were taken from the Pacifics without any enlargement for the increased power of the P2. This applied in particular to the design of the crank axle with all three 21 in cylinders driving on to it. The size of the crankpin was $9\frac{1}{4}$ in diameter but the crank webs were exactly the same as Gresley had used on the K3s in 1920 and in practice this proved to be inadequate for the P2s. There was flexing and vibration of the crank axle under the action of flange forces on the driving wheels and in conjunction with the high piston thrusts. This resulted in frequent failure of the axlebox journals due to rupture of the lubrication film. As with many of the Gresley engines the P2s had their share of big end failure, especially on the piston valved engines with the conjugate gear which at times imposed additional loads on the inside cylinder. All these faults were present to a lesser degree on the Pacifics and the V2s, but on the larger P2s they became crucial. A simple enlargement of the crank pin might indeed have cured many of these troubles. Bulleid used a $9\frac{3}{8}$ in crank pin with 6 in webs on his "Merchant Navy" class Pacifics and a similar crank axle might well have transformed the Gresley engines. As a matter of interest Chapelon used a 9.1 in diameter crank on his four-cylinder compounds while on his post-war three-cylinder 242A1 a 10 in crank pin with $8\frac{1}{2}$ in webs was used. Despite their critics the French compounds were robust enough where it was needed.

As first built No 2001 had infinitely variable cut-offs with the cams operating the admission valves being advanced on scrolls as cut off was reduced, but before the engine had run many miles the scrolls and cams were heavily worn. This may have been due to the extensive use of very short cut offs on the GN main line. The engine was then fitted with an arrangement of stepped cams of stouter design which gave six positions only at 12, 18, 25, 35, 45 and 75 per cent cut off. It might well have been that the engine could have been driven comfortably enough on the regulator on the GNR main line with these limited variations, but control was more difficult on the constant changes of gradient on the NBR main line and this may have been a partial explanation for the periods of brilliant running which were sometimes followed by unaccountable easings. The engine was very free running and if not held back when over the crest of a bank it could accelerate to an uncomfortably high speed in a very short space. In April 1938 *Cock o' the North* emerged from Doncaster with piston valves and A4 nose to conform with Nos 2003–6.

It is thought that the late O. V. S. Bulleid played a considerable part in the designing of the P2s. He always spoke well of *Cock o' the*

North, defending the record of the engine even after many years of retirement. Had the Civil Engineer of the Southern permitted it he would have built an eight-coupled engine instead of the "Merchant Navy" class Pacifics. Opinions differ about the merit of the *Cock o' the North* and the other P2s, but the following chapters will show that they performed feats of haulage which cannot be matched by any other class of British express passenger locomotive. They were fine examples of British locomotive engineering which might perhaps, with a few small modifications, have stood nearer to complete success than posterity realises.

CHAPTER FIVE

The Performance of the P2s— Some Test Running

The new 2-8-2 No 2001 *Cock o' the North* started its working life quietly enough on the GNR section. During the middle of June 1934 it was used on the 11.30 am semi-fast as far as Peterborough, returning on the heavy but easily-timed East Coast express then due into Kings Cross at 4.15 pm. This was work that should have been easy enough for so large a locomotive and on June 19th the new giant had inspired sufficient confidence to attempt a full power test run with the dynamometer car from Kings Cross to the Barkston triangle and back. A special test load of 18 bogies and the dynamometer car was made up. This left Kings Cross at 9.50 am, made a brief stop a Peterborough and was safely stowed away at Barkston before the down "Flying Scotsman" went through. No high downhill speeds were allowed and it is a tribute to the uphill work of the new engine with its vast train that no delay to the "Scotsman" took place. After the passage of the regular expresses No 2001 returned to Kings Cross, again calling briefly at Peterborough.

The 650 ton train passed Finsbury Park in 6 min 6 sec which, although not a record time, had certainly never previously been equalled with so heavy a load. Cut off was brought back from 45 per cent at 20 mph to 20 per cent at the top of the 1 in 105 and halfway up the 1 in 200 to this was increased to 22 per cent, which took the train over the summit at Potters Bar in 17 min 40 sec from the Kings Cross start. The maximum dbhp recorded was 1730 at 58 mph on the brief stretch of down grade near Hornsey. The lowest boiler pressure on the ascent was 195 lb/sq in. After Potters Bar easy running on 10 per cent cut off sufficed to bring the train to a stop at Peterborough in 81 min 46 sec, or in 79 min net, after allowing for a pw check at Yaxley. The highest speed anywhere was 70 mph, which had just been touched at Hatfield and Tempsford. There had been a brief lengthening of the cut off to 15 per cent to take the train up the 1 in 200 to mp 62 at a minimum speed of 53 mph. Contemporary timings by Pacific engines with 500 ton trains show that times of

79 min to Peterborough were common enough, but normal running involved a slower start with times of 20 min, or slightly over, to passing Potters Bar and 25 min to passing Hatfield, though faster running downhill and on the level, with speeds of over 80 mph near Three Counties, restored the balance.

A brief stop of 2 min 25 sec was made at Peterborough and the engine was then extended to some purpose on the rise to Stoke Tunnel. The hp output on the bank was, with little doubt, the highest that had been attained in Britain at that time. The standard of running on the bank was far ahead of normal running by down expresses even with loads far lighter than 650 tons. Even in later years when the A4s were on the scene the record of No 2001 was never surpassed with such a load and in the same speed range and on occasions when the time from Essendine to the summit was closely approached initial speeds were higher and minimum speeds lower. In their chosen optimum speed range of 75–80 mph, however, the A4s occasionally surpassed the performance of *Cock o' the North* in terms of sustained and maximum hp. The run of the P2 remains an LNER record in the lower speed ranges and No 2001 had certainly proved itself to be very strong at moderate speeds. The work on the critical section from Essendine to the summit is best shown in tabular form.

Location	Gradient	Speed	db pull	db horse power
Essendine 88.6 miles	1 in 264	60 mph	4.1 tons	1470
	1 in 550 down			
Mp 90	Level	63 mph	4.5 tons	1690
	1 in 240			
Mp 91	Level	62 mph	4.25 tons	1570
	1 in 200			
Mp 92	1 in 200	60½ mph	4.6 tons	1660
Mp 93	1 in 200	58 mph	4.9 tons	1700
Mp 94	1 in 200	58 mph	5.4 tons	1870
Mp 95	1 in 200	56 mph	5.4 tons	1805
Mp 96	1 in 200	57½ mph	6.1 tons	2090
	Level			
Mp 97	1 in 330	60 mph	5.4 tons	1935
	Level			
Mp 98	1 in 178	57 mph	5.4 tons	1935
Mp 99	1 in 178	57 mph	5.3 tons	1800
Stoke Summit 100.1 miles	1 in 178	56½ mph	5.7 tons	1920

Cut off was advanced from 15 to 20 per cent at mp $89\frac{1}{2}$, to 25 per cent at mp 94 and to 30 per cent near mp $95\frac{3}{4}$; boiler pressure was maintained at between 210 and 200 lb/sq in.

Stoke Summit was cleared in 26 min 43 sec for the 23.7 miles with a pass to pass time of 15 min 14 sec for the 15.3 miles from Tallington to the Summit. Had the train passed Peterborough without stopping Grantham would have been passed in 110 min from Kings Cross. This compared with a contemporary booking of 108 min for the down "Queen of Scots" Pullman which, with an Atlantic and 290 tons, ran at speeds of over 80 mph downhill in order to keep time. A run on a Saturday "Scarborough Flier" with an A3 and 570 tons included a net time of 111 min to passing Grantham. It involved a slow climb to Stoke with a minimum speed of 42 mph, but a maximum of $86\frac{1}{2}$ mph had been reached near Three Counties. The new 2-8-2 had established new standards for hill climbing with heavy loads.

After turning on the Barkston triangle and waiting for a clear path No 2001 set off on its return journey. The start on the sharp curve was, of necessity, slow but it was faster than could reasonably have been expected from a Pacific equally loaded and Grantham was passed at 49 mph. The cutoff was then advanced to 20 per cent and speed dropped to 45 mph at Great Ponton after which it was sustained to the summit. From Stoke Box to Huntingdon the running was very easy with some coasting down the bank. South of Peterborough much of the running was on 12 per cent cut off with a brief increase to 20 per cent up Ripton Bank topped at $45\frac{1}{2}$ mph after 56 mph at Holme. From Biggleswade cut off was advanced to 18 per cent as a preliminary to a magnificent climb to Stevenage. Arlesey was passed at 67 mph and cut off was gradually increased to 30 per cent as *Cock o' the North* blasted its way up to the summit at an absolute minimum of 56 mph. On the short level section through Hitchin a drawbar pull of 5.9 tons and a dbhp of 2100 was recorded at 60 mph, confirming the 2090 near Corby on the down journey. The locomotive proved to be very responsive to opening out and after a 34 mph slack for pw work near Knebworth a cut off of 40 per cent and then 30 per cent brought a rapid acceleration to 68 mph at Welwyn Garden City, after which the engine coasted down to Hatfield where an opening of the regulator and 20 per cent cut off took the train up to Potters Bar in 4 min 38 sec for the 5.0 miles. This had almost been equalled a year earlier by the Pacific engine No 4476 *Royal Lancer* with a load of 660 gross tons and a time of 4 min

41 sec; but the Pacific had passed Hatfield at 74 mph and had topped the bank at 59 mph, while the Mikado had passed Hatfield at under 60 mph and had accelerated uphill to 63 mph—a very significant difference. On the descent steam was shut off at 76 mph near New Barnet and the engine was put into mid gear so lifting the poppet valves off their seats. So free running was the engine under these conditions that speed was still as high as 73 mph as Wood Green was passed. The actual time from passing Grantham to the stop at Kings Cross, including a brief 35 sec stop at Peterborough, was 114 min 15 sec with a start to stop time of 81 min 25 sec for the 76.4 miles from Peterborough. By 1934 standards this meant that any daily schedule except a few very fast bookings with limited loads such as the 7.50 am from Leeds could have been kept with 650 tons and with severely limited downhill speeds.

With these results in mind Cecil J. Allen wrote, with pardonable enthusiasm, of the significance of such good results on the engine's first serious trial. On the figures published the opinion was widely shared, but alas it is doubtful if No 2001 was ever as good again. Now that the years have rolled by and we have the advantage of hindsight some new aspects emerge.

When the test results were first published there were some who remarked on the absence of any details of the coal consumption. In 1934 these people were dismissed as base souls, with loyalties centred elsewhere, who were vainly trying to diminish a well-deserved LNER triumph. Besides, said the Gresley supporters, no coal figures had, up till then, been published for the new LMS Pacifics. We know now why neither company had published the early coal figures for both classes. In 1934, however, we thought the coal consumption of No 2001 must have been light because the engine had been worked over long sections on very short cut offs and on relatively short cut offs even when exceptional hill climbing was being achieved. We know now that nominal cut off positions for poppet-valve engines are not directly comparable with those for piston-valve engines. A relatively short cut off with poppet valves can mean a large volume of steam actually passing into the cylinders with a resulting high coal consumption. It was pardonably but prematurely assumed that, as *Cock o' the North* coasted down some of the most tempting banks, there was a vast reserve of power which could have brought about some really remarkable end to end times, but following later revelations it may well have been that full exploitation of a 50 sq ft grate would have needed oil or mechanical firing. Smaller engines than No 2001 needed two firemen on post-war test runs.

The advantages of poppet valves seemed to be fully established for all time when some of us, with the enthusiasm of youth, read the first accounts of *Cock o' the North*'s running. One of the writers of this book recalls discussing the performance with a member of the technical staff of what was then called Loughborough Engineering College and is now Loughborough University. There was great surprise when he suggested waiting to see what the second engine of the class, with ordinary piston valves, would be like before praising the poppet-valve engine unduly. Following the publication of the test results of 2001 this seemed unduly cautious; surely, one thought, nothing could improve on an engine which coasted downhill at quite high speeds on no steam at all. Later events were destined to prove the wisdom of the older man with his wider experience.

After the test run No 2001 was often seen on the Doncaster turn leaving at 11.4 am and reaching Kings Cross at 1.55 pm. The return journey was on the heavy but easily-timed 4 pm from Kings Cross. It was reported that much of this work was done on 10 per cent cut off with coasting on the down grades. It was assumed that all the coasting and short cut-off work meant something like a rest period for firemen on 2001, but the men found a very different reality. A dynamometer car roll, which has survived from this period, is described in detail by P. J. Coster in *Essays in Steam* (Ian Allan, 1970). This shows short periods of vigorous activity interspersed with easy running and falling boiler pressures. A passenger in the train would have had no conception of the difficulties on the footplate; he would have imagined that the engine was merely playing with the train.

After a period of initial trial running on the GNR section No 2001 was sent to Haymarket Shed, Edinburgh, where it was at first employed on the 9.55 am from Edinburgh to Aberdeen returning on the 3.45 pm. Later it was used on the 2 pm from Edinburgh returning on the very heavy 7.35 pm up "Aberdonian" sleeping car express. This "Aberdonian" job was one of the main reasons why the 2-8-2s had been built. It frequently loaded to 520–550 tons and as a Pacific was not allowed to take a pilot it usually featured a NBR Atlantic assisted by a 4-4-0 "Scott" coupled according to NBR tradition as "inside engine" next to the train. On its first run in Scotland to be recorded in detail *Cock o' the North* made light work of 550 tons by attaining 42 mph on the 1 in 102 gradient, the steepest part of the climb out of Aberdeen, and gaining 8 min on schedule between Aberdeen and Montrose. The exit from Aberdeen was faster than any contemporary timing of double-headed LNER trains and it was only occasionally rivalled by much lighter LMS trains. On August 2nd and 3rd 1934 a huge train of 586 tons tare was worked from Edinburgh to Aberdeen and back. On such a road this was, as so aptly described by P. J. Coster, "an awesome feat indeed". To the outsider the early history of the first P2 seemed to be one of unbroken triumph, but in later years when the viewpoints of the practical men, who had borne the heat and burden of the day, became known then a rather different picture emerged.

In the autumn of 1934 the second P2, No 2002 *Earl Marischal*, was running trial trips on the GNR main line, usually on the 11.4 am from Doncaster and the 4 pm return from Kings Cross. During this period Cecil J. Allen found the engine at the head of the 4 pm with a gross load of 580 tons. The evening was wet and unpleasant turning to fog further north, but No 2002 started from Kings Cross in a way that outclassed anything recorded by a Pacific equally loaded. Finsbury Park was passed in 5 min 51 sec from the start, but this was followed by a most leisurely ascent to Potters Bar with speed falling to 30 mph. It may have been that the vigorous initial start drained the boiler, but another possible explanation was suggested by R. A. H. Weight, who was closely in touch with everything that happened on the GNR main line. It was pointed out that the 4 pm had very tight margins owing to a preceding slow train and a fitted freight, which made any attempt to pass Hatfield before 4.27 pm an invitation for a signal stop. The driver of 2002 had perforce to run easily as he was already ahead of time at the top of Holloway Bank. Once clear of Hatfield *Earl Marischal* ran at quite a high speed with a maximum of 79 mph and with long stretches at over 70 mph, so the train rolled into Peterborough 5 min early in 79 min 56 sec from Kings Cross.

At Peterborough the loss of the North Lincolnshire portion brought the load down to 400 tons and the new 2-8-2 was able to gain time on the short start to stop snippets that followed. Peterborough to Grantham 29.1 miles took 31 min 45 sec, with a minimum of 50 mph at Stoke, against a schedule of 36 min. The downhill section from Grantham to Newark took 15 min 54 sec for the 14.5 miles with a maximum of 77½ mph near Claypole. From Newark the engine accelerated to 68 mph at Carlton and with a minimum of 58½ mph at Markham Summit, brought the train into Retford in 20 min 17 sec for the 18.5 miles against a schedule of 22 min. The fog had thickened considerably and the final run to Doncaster, although within schedule, was of no special note. Over the whole run the new giant had gained 12½ min on schedule. The same issue of *The Railway Magazine* also included Cecil J. Allen's graphic description of the high speed test runs to Leeds and back with No 4472 *Flying Scotsman*. LNER prestige was high as the new year 1935 began, but as interest began to focus on the high speed running, which was destined to reach its brilliant climax with the A4s and the "Silver Jubilee", the 2-8-2s began to take a second place in the hearts and minds of Gresley enthusiasts.

On December 4th 1934 No 2001 was shipped from Harwich on the train ferry on its way to the Locomotive Testing Station at Vitry-sur-Seine. Gresley had long advocated a British testing station of the same kind, but this was destined not to be opened in his lifetime. Photographs appeared in British magazines showing No 2001 on the rollers and on exhibition at the Gare du Nord alongside a Collin Super-Pacific. At the time nothing transpired as to how the engine performed, but the published records of the Chapelon 4-8-0 compounds made British students of locomotive performance realise what high standards the LNER engine was facing in France. The writers are grateful for the help of P. J. Coster, who has had the privilege of discussing the running of *Cock o' the North* with Andre Chapelon, the greatest of all modern steam locomotive engineers. No great success attended the running of No 2001 on the rollers and O. V. S. Bulleid detected the overheating of an axlebox before there was time for any serious trouble to emerge. It appears that the centre line of the axlebox was not in line with the centreline of the frame and the eccentric loading may have ruptured the oil film. The large 2-8-2 with its greater piston thrusts could have used larger axleboxes than the standard A3 pattern.

The lesson was not lost on O. V. S. Bulleid, for he built the "Merchant Navy" class Pacifics with the centre of the axleboxes in line with the centre of the frames and the BR engineers adopted this design feature for the standard range of locomotives. It is a thousand pities that this feature, possibly in conjunction with larger axleboxes, was not incorporated in the four additional P2 class engines built in 1936. The French engineers consoled the LNER party with the news that a number of French locomotives, which had given little or no trouble on the road, suffered from overheating on the rollers. It was suggested that tests should continue with controlled road testing with brake locomotives on the open road.

These tests took place on the Paris Orleans line between Paris and St Pierre-des-Corps. *Cock o' the North* proved to be reasonably economical at low firing rates, but when it was extended to an output in keeping with its size the coal consumption rose at an inordinate rate. It was suggested that a bigger shovel and a bigger firehole door would be needed before the engine reached its full potential. As things were the highest continuous power output was a little over 1900 dbhp, sustained for 35 min. This was little more than had already been achieved by the engine for shorter periods between Tallington and Stoke and between Biggleswade and Stevenage during the 1934 test run. Even 35 min was not a long period by French standards as the Chapelon 4-8-0 No 4701 had sustained a dbhp of 3030 for an hour, fired single-handed by the incredible *Chauffeur* Marty. It is said that boiler pressure on No 2001 was falling, the fireman was tiring towards the end of the 35 min and the engine was throwing fire under the fierce blast. A French fireman, who was used to high firing rates on test runs, was tried but he proved to be no more effective than the Doncaster man.

The coal/dbhp/hr figure was 3.25 lb at the high steaming rate and although this figure would have been considered good on a variable speed dynamometer car test it was high for a constant speed test. The Chapelon 4-8-0, even when extended to a maximum effort, burnt coal at the significantly lower rate of 2.84 lb/dbhp/hr. *Cock o' the North* had hardly proved itself to be the cock of the French farmyard, but when comparison is made with other more modern poppet-valve engines a rather better comparative position emerges. It would appear that poppet valves gave their best performances on compound engines.

We know now that the good cylinder performance of poppet-valve simple engines appeared to go hand-in-glove with disappointing boiler performance, due to the very fierce blast at high power outputs. The standard British Class 8 Pacific, No 71000, proved to be a very heavy coal burner at maximum power output with rather disappointing boiler evaporation rates for an engine of that size. The American Pennsylvania Class T1 4-4-4-4 burnt coal at a reasonable rate, by American standards, of 2.5 lb/ihp/hr at 5525 ihp but this rose to 3.5 lb/ihp/hr at 6666 ihp, while exhaust pressure rose from 11.1 lb/sq in at 5525 ihp, still a very high figure by British standards, to an exceptional 25.9 lb at the maximum effort. The French De Casso 232R class simple Pacifics with poppet valves were reported as being 12 per cent heavier on coal than the 232S class four-cylinder compounds which had the same boiler. In British practice, on smaller engines, the poppet valves only showed a significant economy when replacing the old style short-lap, short-travel, valve gear. They did not show any improvement on good piston-valve engines. Against such a background the results of No 2001 at Vitry can be seen in better perspective.

In the discussion following the paper read to the Institution of Locomotive Engineers by the late B. Spencer in 1947, the late O. V. S. Bulleid claimed that No 2001 reached a hp of 2800 and proved itself to be a very efficient engine in terms of coal/dbhp/hr. It was not stated whether the 2800 hp was drawbar or indicated and a suggestion in the *Stephenson Locomotive Society Journal* that it was more likely to be indicated hp brought an indignant letter from the Society's valued Vice-President, saying that it definitely was drawbar hp. No confirmation of this claim can be found from French sources and no such claim was ever made in contemporary LNER publicity. In fact, in the late Sir Nigel Gresley's Presidential Address to the Institution of Mechanical Engineers in 1936, he claimed that an ihp of 2500–2600, attained by an A4 on Cockburnspath Bank, was a "figure never previously attained in Britain". Although this does not exclude a higher figure on one of his own engines on test in France it is reasonable to suppose that had 2800 dbhp, equivalent to 3200 ihp, been in Sir Nigel's mind at the time he would have been less impressed by the 2600 ihp, 2100 dbhp by the A4. In actual fact the 2100 of the A4 was almost exactly the same as the 2100 attained by the P2 at Corby in 1934, but by 1936 the high-speed Pacifics had completely ousted the Mikados from the limelight. The probability would seem to be that 2800 dbhp, if attained at all, was a brief transitory maximum which would compare very closely with the best short bursts by the LMS Pacific No 6324 *Duchess of Abercorn* when tested in 1939.

Cock o' the North returned from France with suggestions from the French engineers for a number of improvements. Some of these were of a minor nature but some, such as the use of a Zara truck, would have meant a complete redesigning. By Chapelon standards an engine as large as No 2001 would have been capable of over 4000 ihp, but such a power output would be far beyond the needs of the NBR main line. The French engineers were favourably impressed by the solid construction and fine workmanship of the British engine. It would have been a long, difficult road with much costly experiment before the poppet-valve engine could have been brought to complete success, but the potential prize at the end of the road would have been a substantial one. Subsequent events suggest that full success might well have always eluded the most strenuous efforts. Gresley was wise to have accepted the more certain benefits that accompanied the more traditional piston valves of No 2002, which was already showing economy by virtue of its reduced clearance volumes and its infinitely variable cut off. This engine pointed the way to a more modest but more confident success.

It is, however, a great pity that more serious thought was not given to improving the mechanical details of the engines. The frame and axle-box design used by Bulleid on the "Merchant Navy" class together with larger axleboxes and a more robust crank axle assembly might well have transformed the four engines still to be built in 1936. As things were it was the mechanical details rather than the thermo-dynamic performance which brought about the rebuilding of the engines as Pacifics in 1943–4. The eight coupled driving wheels and the 80 tons of adhesion weight were priceless assets which should have been retained if at all possible.

CHAPTER SIX

P2s Performance—
Everyday Work in Scotland

The visit to Vitry had suggested a number of improvements that could with advantage be made to *Cock o' the North*, but by the time the engine was back in Britain interest had shifted to the high-speed programme. There had been rumours while the engines were running in England that No 2002 *Earl Marischal*, with piston valves, was the better engine and this opinion was reinforced by the publication of a series of runs by the P2s in Scotland in the January 1936 *Railway Magazine*. Both engines showed a comfortable mastery over the 530 ton loads but drivers' opinions favoured the piston-valve engine. The cut off of 2002 was infinitely variable, but the poppet-valve engine could only be notched up in large steps. As originally built No 2001 had infinitely variable cut offs and in that condition it had run its famous Kings Cross–Barkston test run. In service the scrolls and cams of the admission valves became heavily worn and these were replaced by stepped cams which gave more coarse control. Nevertheless, as far as concerns actual performance, recorded on the road, the most outstanding runs both in Scotland and England were to the credit of the poppet-valve engine. There is no reason to doubt the ability of 2002 to have equalled the Kings Cross–Barkston test run and the initial trial runs in Scotland, but there is, of course, a difference between a special test performance and everyday running. In England there had been complaints of smoke drifting down because of the very soft blast and extra deflector plates were fitted outside the boiler casing.

The up "Aberdonian" was, perhaps, one of the hardest daily tasks set to a locomotive in Britain in the 1930s, not so much in the sense of high sustained hp but in the difficulty of the various uphill starts. The engine needed to exert a high drawbar pull at the low speeds where steam locomotives were never at their best. Doncaster had an easier task in designing the high speed A4 than in designing the P2 with its strong pull at low speeds. It is not surprising that greater success attended the 100mph engine. If it had been decided to build a steam engine, oil or mechanically fired, to match a "Deltic" diesel then it would have been easier to have matched the 100mph running than to have matched the acceleration from a slack. If the Bulleid "Leader", with its smooth torque and 100 per cent adhesion had ever been brought to success it might have proved to be an ideal engine for such a line as the NBR Aberdeen road.

The timings of the "Aberdonian" were not impressive but they need to be considered in relation to the gradient profile. The NBR had a reputation for a very high standard of punctuality, but there was never any very fast downhill running nor anything very fast on the level section between Arbroath and Dundee. The difficulties lay in the awkward location of many of the stations, which were situated on sharp curves or in the dips or on gradients. The line abounded in speed restrictions. The NBR Atlantics had a reputation for heavy coal consumption in terms of coal in lb/mile but when tested over the Newcastle–Edinburgh route in comparison with NER and GNR Atlantics they proved to be no more extravagant than their contemporaies. The Pacifics had taken some of the burden from the Atlantics, but they had been designed for high-speed running over a straight road with moderate gradients and they were far from being ideal for the Aberdeen road. If the experimental work with boosters on LNER locomotives had been brought to full success a solution to the traffic problem of the NBR main line might have been obtained more cheaply than by building the P2s. As it was the Pacifics performed well enough with loads limited to 420 tons southbound and 480 tons northbound, but this put the 500 ton "Aberdonian" beyond their capacity. The axle loading of a Pacific did not allow them to take pilots, so the Atlantics had to soldier on, with assistance.

The Mikados were well able to take care of the job, making hard sure starts with the advantage of 80 tons of adhesion weight. As an example of what might have been expected every day in the mid 1930s, Cecil J. Allen timed No 2002 with 530 tons starting from Montrose and accelerating to 26½mph on the 1 in 88 and further to 32 mph on the 1 in 132 and finally topping the 1 in 148/121 at 35mph. It mattered little what load was hung on behind the P2s, they would take it away and climb the bank with full mastery. The load limit of 530 tons was influenced as much by the length of station platforms as by the power of the engines.

South of Dundee the engine did not have to face the same difficulties from a series of difficult starts as did its northern partner, but the 1 in 70 ascent to the Forth Bridge with a slack at the bottom was perhaps the most difficult bank of all. Here again the published records showed that the P2s had full mastery.

The comparative strength of the P2s as compared with some of the best starts by four- or six-coupled engines is best shown by the following table of starts from Aberdeen:

4-4-2 No 9868 *Aberdonian*	295 tons	Cove Bay	4.8 miles	9 min 20 sec
2-6-2 No 60824	435 tons	,, ,,	,, ,,	10 min 05 sec
4-6-2 No 60527 *Sun Chariot*	400 tons	,, ,,	,, ,,	9 min 32 sec
2-8-2 No 2001 *Cock o' the North*	550 tons	,, ,,	,, ,,	9 min 23 sec.

The best run in Scotland to be timed in detail was the initial trip of No 2001 between Aberdeen and Montrose:

P2, No 2001 *Cock o' the North*; Load 511 tons tare, 550 tons gross.

Miles		Min	Sec	Speeds
0.0	Aberdeen	00	00	
4.8	Cove Bay	9	23	42 mph
8.2	Portlethen	13	40	
10.4	Newtonhill	15	45	
11.6	Muchalls	17	00	
16.1	Stonehaven	21	36	68 mph
23.3	Drumlithie	30	00	44 mph
27.3	Fordoun	33	33	
30.6	Laurencekirk	36	54	
33.8	Marykirk	40	00	76 mph
35.9	Craigo	41	46	
35.9	Kinnaber Junction	44	10	
		sigs		
40.6	Montrose	50	01	58 min schedule

So far the record of the P2s, as shown by published times, loads and speeds, was a story of unbroken triumph. It appeared that the LNER had solved the problem of operating heavy trains over a difficult road for many years to come. The Mikados maintained the high standards of NBR punctuality with much heavier loads. There are, however, other aspects of locomotive performance. The public sees one and the practical men see the other. The other side of performance with reference to LMS locomotives is discussed at length by E. S. Cox in *Chronicles of Steam* (Ian Allan, 1967). The problems of overall coal consumption, availability, mileages and repair costs are less easily resolved. Some of the discussions at loco-motive inspectors conferences would shock enthusiasts even now if they were made public.

In the years following 1935 the P2s appeared to be maintaining their high standards of running and Cecil J. Allen once wrote that he never timed a bad run by one, but there were hints that all was not

P2 No 2001 *Cock o the North* leaving
Waverley Station at the head of the 9.55am
to Aberdeen in August 1935.   *[J. F. Clay*

Above: P1 No 2394 in original condition heading southwards on the GNR main line with a New England-Ferme Park coal train.

[E. R. Wethersett

P1s at New England Shed
Opposite page, top: No 2393 in original condition and livery complete with booster.
Centre: No 2394 with 62 element superheater and twin snifting valves.
Bottom: No 2394 with standard 32 element superheater and later style LNER livery retaining booster.

[All T. G. Hepburn

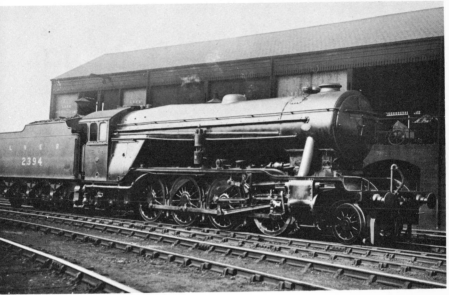

The Latter Days of the P1s

Opposite page:

Top: P1 No 2393 after removal of booster at New England Shed July 10th, 1939.

[J. F. Henton

Centre: No 2394 without booster at work on the Peterborough–London main line.

[E. R. Wethersett

Bottom: No 2394 at the end of its life on the Doncaster scrap road in September 1945, fitted with 220lb A3 type boiler with banjo dome. *[A. F. Cook*

The First P2

Top: No 2001 *Cock o' the North* passing Grantham when almost new in June 1934.

[T. G. Hepburn

Above: No 2001, in original condition, at work on the NBR main line.

[E. R. Wethersett

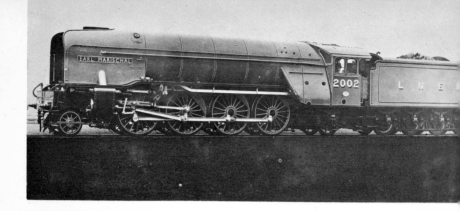

The Second P2

Top: No 2002 *Earl Marischal* in original condition. [LPC

Right: No 2002 *Earl Marischal* at Kings Cross November 7th, 1934. [S. Oborne

Above: No 2002 *Earl Marischal* with additional deflector plates on the down 4pm Leeds and Newcastle express passing Potters Bar on May 5th, 1935. [S. Oborne

Later Variants

Opposite page:

Top: No 2003 *Lord President* on the Up Morning "Parley" at Newark in July, 1936, at the head of a train of early GNR stock. [T. G. Hepburn

Centre: P2 No 2005 with single chimney at the head of a light train near Inverkeithing. [E. R. Wethersett

Bottom: No 2006 rebuilt as A2/2 type Pacific No 60506 at Grantham. [T. G. Hepburn

The final P2 No 2006 *Wolf of Badenoch* at work on the NBR main line. This engine had a boiler with a longer combustion chamber.   [*E. R. Wethersett*

The First Green Arrows
Opposite page:
Top: No 4771 *Green Arrow* at Grantham on an up express in July 1936. This was one of its earliest express passenger trips.
[*T. G. Hepburn*

Bottom: The 4pm express from Kings Cross passing Ganwick hauled by V2 No 4791.
[*C. R. L. Coles*

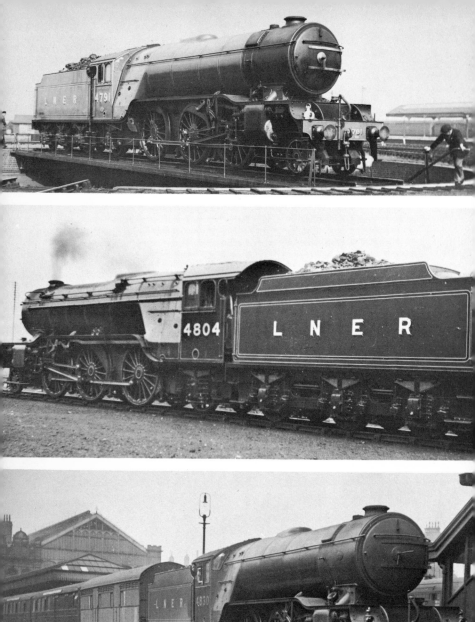

Pre-war V2s
Opposite page:
Top: V2 No 4791 on Grantham turntable
10-4-1939. *[J. F. Henton*
Centre: V2 No 4804 with MLS regulator and
NER type tender. *[W. B. Yeadon*
Bottom: V2 No 4830 on up Manchester–
London at Nottingham Victoria. This was
the first regular GCR turn worked by a V2.
[T. G. Hepburn

The GNR Main Line
Top: V2 No 4774 on up Excursion train of
M&GNR stock passing Marshmoor.
[E. R. Wethersett
Above: V2 No 4789 at the head of the down
"Scotch Goods". *[LPC*

Opposite: V2 No 853 on a Leeds–Doncaster train consisting of a quintuple ex GNR articulated set passing Beeston Junction.

[Eric Treacy

Three Figure Numbers

Above: In evening sunshine the down *Aberdonian* near Welwyn Viaduct headed by V2 No 899.

[F. R. Hebron

Top: V2 No 3663 passing Ganwick with the down Cleethorpes in 1946.   *[W. M. Early*
Above: V2 No E.891 leaving York on a Bristol Newcastle express.   *[Eric Treacy*

Black V2s

Opposite page:

Top: V2 No 813 at Kings Cross 18-2-47 showing the small smoke deflection device on the smokebox.   *[C. C. B. Herbert*

Centre: V2 No 60813 on up freight near Little Wymondly. The engine is in the LNWR type BR livery and has small smoke shields.   *[E. R. Hebron*

Bottom: V2 No 60916 at Doncaster Works 8-1950 in BR black livery with LNWR type lining.   *[J. F. Clay*

V2s on Named Expresses
Top: V2 No 60909 leaving Holbeck with the up *White Rose*.   *[Eric Treacy*

Above: V2 No 60982 leaving Leeds with the down *Queen of Scots*.   *[Eric Treacy*

well with the Mikados. The late J. N. Maskelyne, President of the Stephenson Locomotive Society, gave a lecture in the late 1930s at a number of Society centres, entitled "Locomotive Types That Have Failed to Fulfil Expectations". It was with horror that Gresley enthusiasts found that *Cock o' the North* was included among some pretty disreputable company. Consolation was sought in the fact that the speaker was a self-confessed admirer of the GWR and that his remarks were directed against the poppet-valve engine, not against the piston-valve examples which were reputedly much better. Confirmation of the superiority of the piston-valve engines came with the building of Nos 2003–2006 in 1936 and the rebuilding of 2001 to conform in 1938.

The building of additional P2 class engines meant that most of the heavy trains were well cared for, but it also meant that the big engines were, at times, under-utilised on very light loads of six bogies. When a very large engine is employed on such work capital is badly utilised and coal is wasted moving a heavy engine before any revenue-earning haulage takes place, but at least the repair costs are not inflated as much as when a small engine is thrashed. When No 2001 first went to Scotland in 1934 it was used on through workings between Edinburgh and Aberdeen. When No 2002 was also available engine-changing at Dundee was introduced, but later through working with changes of crew at Dundee was reintroduced. During the war it is rumoured that under the cover of darkness one ventured south of Edinburgh into England. At first it was claimed that the engines would be used on the Waverley route but there is no evidence that this ever took place. In 1941 the Mikados, which had been suffering like other express engines from lack of care about external appearance, were repainted in wartime unlined black with letters NE only on the tender. Before the end, No 2004 lost the fairing in front of the cylinders.

In 1941 most enthusiasts found themselves in a world where aircraft loomed larger in their lives than trains and it was only occasionally that news of locomotives filtered through. In 1941 the RCTS published an excellent statistical history of LNER locomotives written by Messrs Prentice and Proud. The book was a reprint of a series of articles in the *Railway Observer*. The final paragraph on the P2s contained a suggestion that the engines had not fulfilled expectations in regular service and that they had to a large extent been replaced by the V2 class which were easier to maintain. This must have meant a reduction in maximum loads because a V2, at its

best, could never have been expected to equal the uphill performances
of the P2s. In July 1942 Cecil J. Allen wrote that the P2s had been
relatively one of the less successful of the Gresley designs. The same
article brought the first published suggestion that the Mikados could
possibly be brought south to try their hands at the haulage of 700 ton
trains between Kings Cross and York. It was suggested that the
straight main line would have been more to their liking than the
sharp curves of the Edinburgh–Aberdeen road, which had been a
major cause of their troubles.

The P2s had been operated with success in pre-war days in terms
of loads, times and speeds but the task had not been an easy one.
With regular crews and relatively moderate mileages and skilled
care at the sheds they had managed, but when wartime conditions
worsened a more unhappy situation arose. As call-up proceeded it
was difficult for the railways to keep enough skilled men for locomotive maintenance and those that did remain each had to do the
work of several under increasingly difficult conditions. These un-
favourable conditions reacted against the efficient operation of all
engines; several classes of immaculate reputation before the war were
cutting a sorry figure after a few years of war and it is not surprising
that a small class of highly specialised locomotives were less than
popular.

It was, however, with considerable shock that we learned that
Edward Thompson intended to convert the P2s to Pacifics. This led
to a storm of controversy which makes it difficult, even today, to
discuss the question on a logical rather than on an emotional basis.
The supporters of Thompson suggest that Gresley built the Mikados
with the aim of emulating the success of Chapelon rather than with a
view to the difficulties of the road and that he stubbornly refused to
alter the design once they were built. This left his successor, they
claim, with no alternative but to scrap or drastically to rebuild the
engines. The Gresley enthusiasts maintain that the troubles which
beset the P2s were largely imaginary and that Thompson rebuilt the
P2s solely to have the excuse to try out his own ideas of divided drive
and separate sets of valve gear on a large three-cylinder engine
during the period of wartime restrictions.

Some support for the Thompson viewpoint came in September
1956 when the *Trains Illustrated* magazine published an article by
"Toram Beg", a title which hid the identity of a famous Haymarket
driver. "Toram Beg" had handled the Gresley A3 Pacific *Spearmint*
with distinction for many years, but he evidently did not have the

same affection for the Mikados. He complained of constant trouble from overheated axleboxes, from leaking steam pipe joints and of excessive strain on the firemen owing to the heavy coal consumption. It was suggested at the time that "Toram Beg" had overstated his case and to this he replied that his practical experience with the class was sufficient for him to be considered as a reliable witness. He conceded the strength of the P2s, saying that drivers never bothered to count the coaches knowing that the engine would be master of any load, but he considered the strength to be obtained at a prohibitive cost.

It has been suggested that the P2s "spread the track", but this was denied by a former LNER locomotive engineer closely associated with the engines. He did, however, agree with the published claim that there were derailments on some curved roads in shed yards. In this connection the P2s were in no sense alone. There were a number of derailments of Pacifics in Kings Cross locomotive yard, especially in their early days, and a number of BR 2-10-0s were off the road in Woodford GC yard. There appears to have been no case of a dangerous derailment of a P2 at speed, which is more than can be said for some locomotive classes that are never criticised.

No official figures for the coal consumption of the P2s were ever published, but there have been suggestions that the average consumption was in the order of 80–90lb/mile, while considerably higher figures were associated with No 2001 on its 600 ton test runs in Scotland. These figures are, of course, unofficial and the figure of 80–90lb was probably not excessive when due regard was had to the nature of the road and the fact that the only alternative was double-heading. It was also claimed that when the load was less than 450 tons it was cheaper to use a Pacific, but again no official figures were published for the Pacifics. The tragedy is that we have no test figures for the piston-valve engines, which it was claimed were lighter on coal than the poppet-valve No 2001.

Just what can be believed from the many contradicting opinions which have been printed about these engines? While it is recognised that there is no hope, nor any desire, to change viewpoints now fully entrenched it is submitted that the following points are beyond question:

1. The P2s did all that was required in terms of load haulage on the gradients.

2. The P2s fell short of a desirable standard of availability and gave

trouble with overheating. These troubles could be contained in peacetime, but they made the engines almost impossible to operate in wartime.

3. When rebuilt as Pacifics they were unable to match the uphill performances of the original 2-8-2s.

In view of the position which he inherited in 1941 Thompson was in a difficult situation and he was justified in taking some drastic action with the engines. He was, however, in error in thinking that the eight-coupled engines could be replaced by any Pacific. There was perhaps some justification in thinking that a Pacific with a 50 sq ft grate and 40000 lb of tractive effort could manage the difficulties of the Aberdeen road, for the LMS Pacific No 6234 *Duchess of Abercorn* had run test trains of 600 tons over steep gradients in 1939, achieving in the process dbhps at least as high as any recorded by one of the LNER P2s. This was, however, arguing from the particular to the general: although the high hps by 6234 were authentic recordings, there was a great difference between an all-out test run and the average daily standard of running. There were times, in ordinary service, when free-steaming "Duchesses" had to take bankers or lose time on the northern banks with loads far less than the 610 ton test train taken by No 6234.

The Mikado rebuilt as a Class A2/2 Pacific was as liable to slip as any 4-6-2. At times the A2/2s would climb the banks in good style, especially if the foot of a bank could be approached at high speed, but more frequently slipping reduced the effective capacity of the engine to little more than that of the smaller V2s. An official LNER publication of 1947 claimed that fears that the reduced adhesion weight would make the Pacifics less effective on the banks had proved to be groundless, but this must have caused some cynical comments in the running sheds. "Toram Beg" quoted a fellow driver who said that the rebuilds would slip on Portobello Sands. The preponderance of evidence supports the driver.

The reputation of Thompson might now rest on a more certain foundation had there been no attempt to use the rebuilt Pacifics on the former P2 duties. It might have been wiser to have adapted the train loads to the V2s' Scottish maxima and to have sent the rebuilds south into England for work on flatter gradients right from the start. Pacific engines are at their best in high-speed running and the best performances ever recorded by the A2/2s were with moderate loads between Darlington and York. One was once timed at 85mph on the level interlude between the gradients which extended from Dundee to Arbroath. It was no consolation for the crew of an engine troubled by slipping on the ascent to the Forth Bridge to be told that it would be a fast engine on the level.

In due course the A2/2s were sent into England and were stationed at New England and York sheds, rather unfashionable dwellings for former Scottish aristocrats. They were replaced in Scotland by the Peppercorn A2s, which had a shorter wheelbase, but by then the maximum loads were around 450 tons against the 550 tons once worked by the P2s. The Peppercorn engines did quite well, but it was found that Scottish area engines needed more attention to frames during overhaul at Doncaster than those of the same class stationed in England. This was a significant indication of the difficulties of the Aberdeen road. A powerful diesel locomotive should have been ideal for the Edinburgh–Aberdeen road, but since modernisation the tendency has been towards faster but lighter trains.

Towards the end the P2s were running half the yearly average mileage of the Scottish area V2s and they were spending three times as many days out of service, but it would appear that rather better mileage figures had been recorded in peacetime. In the light of such figures there seems to have been little case for keeping the engines in wartime service as they were. The question, however, may be asked whether a less drastic rebuilding could have allowed their retention as 2-8-2s. Thompson supporters point out that Reid had deliberately chosen the 4-4-2 wheel arrangement instead of the apparently more logical 4-6-0 because of the curvature of the NBR main line. Gresley enthusiasts replied to this by pointing out that, overseas, eight-coupled engines were employed with success on lines with even more severe curvature. If the 2-8-2 arrangement had been retained there could have been some improvement from larger bearings or possibly roller bearings, from a more robust crank axle assembly and from a redesigned middle big end. The Bulleid-designed frames with centralised axleboxes coupled with the use of Swindon method of optical lining up could have helped and it would, very possibly, have prevented the hot axlebox detected by Bulleid at Vitry. If a more drastic rebuilding was accepted then the whole front end of the engine might have been re-designed to include the Krause Helmholtz or the Zara leading truck.

All such suggestions are, of course, pure conjecture. In actual fact No 2005 emerged from Doncaster in January 1943 rebuilt as a

Pacific and the remaining five followed in 1944. So it was that this bold experiment in locomotive engineering came to a rather inglorious end. As *Cock o' the North* made its debut and ran its exciting initial test run in 1934; few people could have imagined that it was destined to suffer a minor rebuilding and a major rebuilding all in the space of ten years. Controversy about these engines will continue, but one thing stands out beyond any shadow of doubt. The strength of the Mikados, at low speeds on steep gradients, can never be questioned. It needs to be repeated loudly and clearly that, in everyday, regular service, in all weathers, there was no type of British express locomotive that could take away a 550–600 ton train from an uphill start and climb the bank with equal certainty. That particular facet of supremacy must remain the epitaph of the class.

CHAPTER SEVEN

The History of the 2-6-2 Type

There was ample justification for selecting the 2-6-2 type for mixed traffic duty. It found support in world locomotive history, but if very high speeds were contemplated then, unless a better engine than had so far been built to this wheel arrangement was intended, the 2-6-2 type was more than a little suspect. In the United States the type was less numerous than the 2-8-2, but it had a more exciting and romantic history. Some very fast running was undoubtedly performed, in the US, by 2-6-2 locomotives. The name "Prairie" suggested that it found its main role on the plains and it was on relatively easy gradients that the type rose to fame.

American locomotive builders exported the type before it became popular in its own country and the 2-6-2 was used in New Zealand where one was timed by Charles Rous Marten at 64mph, a remarkable speed for driving wheels of 4ft 1in diameter. Rous Marten wrote later that the engine was running at its maximum possible speed. For the 3ft 6in gauge this must have remained a world record from the mid-1880s to the 1930s.

In the US the 2-6-2 type was built continuously from 1901 until 1910 for both main-line freight and passenger service. The 2-4-2 type, once so popular in America, developed into the 4-4-2 and the 2-6-2. Both types allowed for the use of the wide firebox, but the 4-4-2 had better riding qualities to be set against the superior adhesion of the 2-6-2. The Lake Shore and Michigan Southern Railway was the one on which the 2-6-2 was most likely to succeed as the "water level route" was free from sharp curves or steep banks for the whole distance of 510 miles from Chicago to Buffalo. The Lake Shore introduced the 2-6-2 type first in 1901 and these engines had a brief but most exciting spell in the limelight on high-speed service. The Lake Shore was one of those that later made up the New York Central; it was responsible for the western end of the line on which ran the world-famous "Twentieth Century Limited".

In 1905 the New York–Chicago run was accelerated to an 18 hour timing and 2-6-2s were used at the western end and Atlantics further east. On June 18th 1905 the first eastbound train left

Chicago behind Lake Shore 2-6-2 No 4695 with 6ft 8in driving wheels, 200lb pressure, piston valves driven by inside Stephensons gear and of course, in 1905, no superheater. The load was only four cars, but the 101 miles from Chicago to Elkhart were run in 89 min a start to stop average of 68 mph. The Lake Shore 2-6-2s which worked the train on its first 18 hr run each arrived at their changing point a few minutes early and each one ran its section in better than even time. From Buffalo onwards the Atlantic engines of the eastern partner were ordered to keep to the schedule, so it appeared to the world that the 2-6-2s were faster. The day's running was a great boost to the Prairie type locomotive for high-speed express work.

The success of these engines led to the introduction of a series of larger 2-6-2s in 1905. These engines were based on a 55 sq ft grate instead of the 48 sq ft grate of the earlier engines and the larger boiler was pitched higher. The piston valves remained inside, but they were driven by outside Walschearts gear instead of inside Stephensons link motion. That very able writer the late Rev J. R. Howden, in his *Boy's Book of Locomotives*, described these engines as the largest passenger locomotives in the world but almost before his book reached the shops, they had been replaced by Pacifics. The larger 2-6-2s established a great reputation for very high speed when they made a number of fast runs with mail trains carrying British Government Australian mail. When these had been delayed further west great efforts were made to catch the Cunard liners waiting at New York. As with many high-speed runs at this period of American history it is impossible at this late date to be sure just where history and folk lore overlap, but it would appear that start to stop average speeds of over 70 mph were achieved over long distances. Claims, based on train despatchers' sheets, suggested that speeds of over 100 mph were recorded behind both classes of Prairies, but the very nature of the long, evenly graded route suggests that fast times would be made by sustained high averages rather than by sudden surges up to high maximum speeds.

At one time that story of the Prairie class locomotives on the Lake Shore line seemed to be one of unbroken success, but when the true facts could be seen in perspective the disadvantages of the type emerged in sharper relief. Beyond question it was the instability of the 2-6-2s at high speed that caused such an early replacement by Pacifics. There were a number of derailments at high speed and these were thought to be due to the light loading of the two-wheeled leading truck, which meant an undue dependence for guidance on the leading pair of driving wheels. There were occasions when the leading pair of driving wheels left the rails and bumped along for a while on the sleepers before re-railing themselves. If so much worry was caused by the instability of the 2-6-2s on the Lake Shore main line, which was virtually without sharp curves or heavy grades, then the type would be even less successful for other railroads. The Chicago Burlington & Quincy built a class of medium speed 2-6-2s with 5 ft 9 in driving wheels, but in general the American 2-6-2s were fast freight engines with 5 ft 3 in wheels. The American total of 1700 2-6-2s, with only about 1000 of these intended for main-line service, was in contrast to the vast hordes of 2-8-2s.

It was on the continent of Europe that the 2-6-2 type was constructed in the greatest numbers, with Russia and Italy in particular being prolific users of the type. Some of the popularity of the 2-6-2 in Europe was due to the Krauss-Helmholtz truck and copies of it in countries other than Germany. This device allowed slight sideways movement of the leading coupled axle, which was combined in a species of bogie with the leading pony truck. There were, of course, joints in the leading coupled rods to allow this. It will never be known if such an invention would have given stability to engines which needed to run as fast as the Lake Shore Prairies.

The Russians built a total number of around 4000 2-6-2s, the largest number built in any country. There were a number of stages in the development of the 2-6-2 over the years, but the same basic pattern of performance was common to all. These tall engines would pull very heavy loads at moderate speeds over vast distances. They broke no records, but they served the Czar and later the Soviet Union from 1911 until well into the 1960s and proved themselves faithful servants to both masters.

The Italians built 2-6-2s from 1907 until 1927, at first as four-cylinder compounds but later as four-cylinder simples, in each case with one valve chest arranged to serve a pair of cylinders. They had a low axle loading, which gave them a most valuable range of route availability; but as was the case with the Italian 2-8-2s, they were never unduly vigorous in their movements. As time went by they received a number of modifications including Caprotti valve gear and Franco-Crosti boilers. The Italian 2-6-2s had the Zara or "Italian Truck" which combined the leading wheels and the first pair of driving wheels in a form of bogie similar to the Krauss Helmholtz truck.

There were relatively few 2-6-2s in Germany before the first LNER 2-6-2 was built in 1936, but in the post-war world the type was built in large numbers with 105 in West Germany and 113 in East Germany. These standard 2-6-2s were intended as a replacement for the numerous Class 38 Prussian 4-6-0s. German drivers were not entirely convinced that the new engines were better than the old, but the standard 2-6-2s did good work with heavy loads at moderate speeds.

The first Gresley V2 built in 1936 was not the first British example of the type, but the first engine did little or no serious work. This was the experimental Paget 2-6-2 with its unique boiler and sleeve-valve engine. The many novel features of this engine lie outside the scope of this book and those interested are referred to *Derby Works and Midland Locomotives* by Brian Radford (Ian Allan, 1971), but the point of interest lies in its wheel arrangement. It was at first intended to be a 4-6-0, but the final design was a 2-6-2. This does not appear to have been any disadvantage as one of the few points in the engine's performance which drew enthusiastic comment was its smooth running at speed, which was described as being "Like a Spinner." This was the highest praise in a Midland man's vocabulary at that time.

There had been rumours of a Churchward 2-6-2 in the early years of the 20th Century, but nothing has emerged to give proof of this project. Charles Rous Marten had a high regard for the type as a result of his high-speed run in his native New Zealand and he may have hoped that Churchward was the British engineer most likely to oblige. It is well known that he made a close study of American practice as he developed his standard range of locomotives. A British equivalent of the Lake Shore Flyers might have distinguished itself on Brunel's Old Main Line, but the thought of one running a blinder down Wellington Bank, with its curves, makes one shudder.

When the first three-cylinder GNR 2-6-0 appeared in 1920 some people were disappointed that it was not the rumoured 2-6-2. Again nothing has, so far, been published to give a firm basis for this rumour, but it is known that, in 1919, there were plans for a 2-6-2 tank engine for the Kings Cross suburban services. The success of the 2-6-0 in high-speed service on the GNR led to a further rumour while the first Gresley Pacific was being designed in 1922. Many expected a 2-6-2, but if Gresley was following the practice of the Pennsylvania RR there was little reason for him to favour the 2-6-2 rather than the Pacific. In 1905 the Pennsylvania, possibly influenced by the initial success of the Lake Shore Prairies, ordered a pair of 2-6-2s from the

American Locomotive Company, but the design was not destined
to become a standard type for them. It is said that doubts were
raised over its stability at speed on a line with more curves than the
Lake Shore. Britain had to wait until 1936 before a 2-6-2 tender
engine was built for everyday regular service.

The Southern Railway might well have built a 2-6-2 at about the
same time as the LNER. In 1933 R. E. L. Maunsell was thinking of
a Pacific design based on a "Lord Nelson" for the heavy boat trains
on the former South Eastern section. The Pacific was rejected by the
Civil Engineer and thoughts turned to a 2-6-2, which might be
regarded as a development of the Maunsell three-cylinder 2-6-0s of
Class U1. Had this engine been built it would have been very
similar to a V2 in size and general dimensions, but it would have had
three independent sets of valve gear instead of derived motion. The
SR 2-6-2 suffered the same fate as the Pacific, as it was vetoed by the
Civil Engineer. So it was that Gresley's *Green Arrow* was the first
British 2-6-2 tender engine to be multiplied for regular service and
the Southern had to wait five more years for the appearance of their
large engine in the shape of the Bulleid Pacifics.

It may be said that in his choice of the 2-6-2 for heavy main-line
mixed traffic work Gresley was following a well-tried precedent,
but if high-speed running of the type that fell to the lot of the V2s
had been intended, then it might be asked if it was wise, in view of
the experience of the Lake Shore and Michigan Southern, to persist
with the type. Against this it could be argued that more was known
about locomotive suspension in 1936 than in 1901 and the LNER
2-6-2s were better vehicles than the Lake Shore Prairies. The choice
of the 2-6-2 for the type of work which would have fallen to the
smaller 2-6-2s of the V4 class first built in 1941 could more easily be
defended on the grounds of stability. It is interesting to examine the
record of the LNER 2-6-2s in the light of world experience.

CHAPTER EIGHT

The Gresley V2s

In 1936 the reputation of Gresley and the LNER was very high. The late 1920s and early 1930s had seen the zenith of the GWR; by the middle 1930s popular fancy had turned to the LNER. The P2s had appeared in 1934 and their reputation was largely untarnished, while late in 1934 and early in 1935 *Flying Scotsman* and *Papyrus* had made their spectacular high-speed runs. Early in 1935 we heard the first hints of the coming of the V2s when the LNER announced its intention of building some engines for "heavy long-distance work of the type not yet finally decided upon". This gave rise to joyous expectancy among East Coast supporters and wild rumours began to circulate.

Despite its popularity the LNER, as judged by the economist rather than by the enthusiast, was in a far less happy position than the GWR which, thanks to the forward looking policy of Churchward, had modernisation in depth while Gresley had only had the money to top up the LNER locomotive stock. At times of heavy traffic on the East Coast route K3s were made to run faster than was comfortable and aging Atlantics were made to work harder than was desirable. The need for better running mates for the Pacifics had to be faced.

In 1947 the paper read by B. Spencer to the Institution of Locomotive Engineers lifted the veil on some of the designs proposed at the time. The first was a 2-6-4-4 with the tender articulated to the engine. It was proposed to use the K3 boiler and driving wheels of 6 ft 2 in diameter. This idea was abandoned and having rejected the idea of enlarging a K3 Doncaster then considered reducing a Pacific. Two designs were considered, a 4-6-0 and the 2-6-2, which was finally selected. The proposed 4-6-0 was described in some accounts as a "Super 'Sandringham' ", but actually it could better be called a shortened Pacific. There was, at one time, the possibility that both 4-6-0 and 2-6-2 would have been built as the 4-6-0 was attractive for use on lines with short turntables, but when the 2-6-2 established itself the 4-6-0 was abandoned. There is no reason why the latter design with a shortened A3 boiler and A4-type cylinders should not have equalled the LMS "Royal Scots", but it would have needed to have ridden better at speed than the D49s, the B17s or the K3s to have been popular.

It may be asked why, in view of the experience with the high-speed 2-6-2s in the US, Gresley chose this wheel arrangement but the building of a 2-6-2 was a logical compromise between Pacific and K3 2-6-0. It was a step fully in the GNR tradition, for had not Stirling built 2-2-2s to strengthen the ranks of his 4-2-2s? In his excellent biography of Sir Nigel Gresley, F. A. S. Brown published a line drawing of Stirling 2-2-2 No 234 made by Gresley at the age of thirteen. Now, at that age he can hardly have imagined that one day he would himself wear the mantle of Stirling and when the time came for him to be apprenticed he went to Crewe, not to Doncaster. We are told that, when worried over the steaming of the original No 10000, Gresley suggested that the blast pipe design of the 1003 class eight-footers should be re-examined. It is well known with what enthusiasm he followed the fortunes of the resurrected eight-footer No 1 in 1938. If, as it would appear, Gresley was an admirer of the Stirling engines, then it would appear to have been wholly logical to have supplemented the 4-6-2s with some 2-6-2s.

The first V2s materialised in June 1936, when, with true Gresley showmanship, the technical press were shown *Lord President*, *Green Arrow* and a V3 tank. The hearts of East Coast supporters were high in the summer of 1936: they had new engines, 113 mph by *Silver Fox*, epic runs by *Solario* and the veteran Atlantic No 4404, some encouraging statistical results from the "Silver Jubilee" streamliner and not a hint of any reply from their old rivals. All that came that summer from Swindon was a "Dukedog" and, had it not been for some stout hillclimbing by "Princesses" on the down "Mid-day Scot" Doncaster would have monopolised attention.

The new 2-6-2 was well received. There was no nonsense about streamlining and here was a good looking engine in the classical A3 tradition. It had originally been the intention to number the engine 637 and a photograph as such with curved nameplates appears in F. A. S. Brown's book, but the engine made its debut as No 4771 with a straight nameplate on the side of the smokebox, though 637 remained stamped on the motion. The name *Green Arrow* was inspired by a contemporary scheme for express parcels which, it was hoped, would counter road competition. The name was most appropriate for the fast goods services on which the new engines were to be mainly employed.

There were no risky design features and good performance was confidently expected. At this time the "Jubilee" class 4-6-0s were under a cloud and Stanier was facing criticism for ordering so many straight from the drawing board. Consequently there was approval of Gresley's caution in building only five V2s and scattering them among a number of sheds to prove their worth in varied conditions of service. The original intention may not have been to have built as many as 184 and had finances continued to be restricted more rebuilding of old engines would have continued alongside a minimum of new construction. As things happened the financial position was eased slightly by the Railways Agreement Act, which authorised a Government Guaranteed Loan, and by a small but very welcome hint of better traffics.

The new 2-6-2s were fitted with 6 ft 2 in driving wheels similar to those used on the P2 class 2-8-2s but the wheels were more widely spaced than on the Pacifics, with the result that the coupled wheelbase was 15 ft 6 in against 14 ft 6 in on the express engines. The axle loading on the second and third pairs of driving wheels was the same as that of the A3s and A4s but it was very slightly less on the leading pair. The two-wheeled leading truck took a weight of 11 tons, while the rear pair of carrying wheels with the usual Cartazzi axleboxes carried a weight of 16½ tons more than an A3 but less than an A4. The total engine weight was less than an A3's but more than that of the 180 lb pressure Pacifics. The route availability was no better than that of an A3 class Pacific. The engine had filled the bill for "heavy long-distance work" but it was never to be a mixed traffic design with wide scope. It was destined to find its role in the main lines. This was recognised by the RA9 classification.

The use of the 2-6-2 wheel arrangement with relatively large wheels, widely spaced, allowed for the use of a large boiler with a wide firebox. The boiler was similar to that used on the A3 class Pacifics but the barrel was 2ft shorter. The reduction in length was in the forward parallel portion of the boiler; the rear portion was tapered just as was standard practice in other large Gresley boilers. The banjo dome with steam collector, as used on the final batch of A3s, the P2s and the A4s, was fitted. This device was provided for the purpose of reducing priming. The engine had a slightly greater superheating surface than the A3 class, 680 sq ft, but the same boiler pressure of 220 lb/sq in was used. The smokebox was similar to the A3's with single blast and no experiments with double blast were made in Gresley's lifetime.

The cylinders were of the A4 pattern with the same 9 in piston valves and the same "internal streamlining" of steam and exhaust passages. The term "internal streamlining" needs a little qualification. Steam can go round corners, for it does so in superheater elements. Carbonisation, of course, was not limited to engines with large ports and passages; it also happened in the earlier designs with restricted passages and then the effects would be worse. It was a demonstrable fact that locomotives whose exhaust passages had been opened out in the Chapelon manner were more free running than earlier designs.

The V2 cylinders were made in a monobloc casting instead of the separate castings used on the A3s. A feature of Gresley cylinder design was that particular care was taken to reduce clearance volumes by careful shaping of the inlet steam belt to provide the minimum area necessary for flow. The top half of the belt was accordingly of reduced section compared with the ample areas often unnecessarily provided in other locomotives. The Gresley piston was forged in one piece and was specially shaped to fit the clearance spaces. A modest clearance volume of 7.9 per cent was achieved on the A4 and V2 in comparison with figures of 12.5 per cent on some contemporary locomotives of similar size and power. The low clearance volume enabled a low lead of $\frac{1}{8}$ in to be provided. All these features were conducive to high cylinder efficiency, as was destined later to be proved under test conditions.

The connecting rods were fairly short and, in contrast to those of the Pacifics, they were of equal length. In other respects the V2s had most of the classical Gresley features. The 2 and 1 gear was located in front of the cylinders and judged by the V2s' beat, which may still be heard on several gramophone records available for sale, the effects of the Gresley gear seemed to be at its worst on this class. It has been suggested that their shorter connecting rods made for greater errors on the outside motion which was multiplied and transferred to the inside cylinder. The V2s generally had rather higher superheat than most of the other Gresley classes and this increased the valve spindle expansion effects. It was alleged that Darlington works did not in fact make any allowance for expansion when setting the valves and the majority of the V2s were built and shopped there. Significant improvements to the Gresley gear were made later following the introduction of Swindon optical lining up methods at Doncaster. Undoubtedly Gresley gear was at its best with the levers behind the cylinders, as in the D49 and B17 classes.

The cylinders all drove on one axle with the middle cylinder slightly inclined. The inside crank was advanced 9 deg relative to the outside cranks to compensate for this. It has been suggested that this hardly helped starting when the engine was stopped in certain positions and despite the reputation gained by the class for the heroic haulage of 700–800 ton wartime loads, they were not really suited for such work and much straining and setting back was needed to get these loads on the move. The V2s were happiest as understudies to the Pacifics; they were racehorses rather than cart-horses. Cut off was limited to 65 per cent in full gear and this again assisted fast running rather than brisk starting. They had the classical Gresley features including vertical screw reversers with vacuum-operated clutch, pull-out regulator handles on each side, cable-operated cylinder cocks and Pacific-type axleboxes. They were, in fact, shortened Pacifics with a swing axle pony truck instead of a leading bogie.

The standard six-wheeled tender holding 7½ tons of coal and 4200 gallons of water was provided. Most of the engines had the later pattern tender with the flush sides, but a small number of those built at Darlington had the older pattern with stepped-out copings from other engines. The later tenders had a higher front-end shield designed to give better protection to the enginemen. Among those having the stepped-out tender tops were Nos 4804/8, which had the MLS multiple valve regulator with external rods. These were later removed, but this type of regulator was subsequently used on some Peppercorn A2s and on the BR standard Pacifics. It is not known just why the experimental fitting was removed from the V2s since there had been some trouble from the standard regulator fitted to them. This was of the Gresley balanced double-seat type and apart from being stiff to operate it suffered from steam leakage from the lower seat. This could be dangerous while engines were standing in shed yards and the cylinder drain cocks had to be left open for steam to blow through. It was not only a nuisance on account of noise, but it made the class very unpopular on other Regions and at one time the WR seriously considered banning them from their lines. Subsequently a modified regulator valve with single seat and pilot valve similar to the former NER Darlington type was fitted. This allowed more sensitive handling.

The frames were 1⅛ in thick and frame performance was very good and relatively trouble-free. There had been considerable development of frames since the early days of the Pacifics when frame cracking was frequently due, among other things, to the holes made in the frames to reduce weight. On the V2s the monobloc casting added a considerable degree of stiffening to the front end. Compared with some other multi-cylinder designs, including the Thompson replacements, which lacked frame stiffness at the front end due to the staggered cylinders, the V2s were a model of good practice.

Mechanical lubrication was employed on the V2s after Gresley had experimented with the Detroit hydrostatic type on his earlier Pacifics. Steam atomisation was used for cylinder and valve lubrication. The Gresley piston valve had four narrow rings per head with the valve edge cut back to the front ring and with the high degree of superheat, a certain amount of carbonisation occurred, upsetting valve events, after the edge was carboned up. Some trouble from carbonisation was, of course, normal with all steam locomotives.

In service the class was reasonably popular with the crews and in pre-war days, with the track in good condition, they were considered to be a good riding design. Up to the outbreak of war they had run at speeds as high as any required from the Lake Shore & Michigan Prairies mentioned earlier but the two-wheeled leading truck on the British engines was free from suspicion. They rode well at high speeds on the excellent GN main line and they were well thought of at lower speeds on the Edinburgh–Aberdeen road. There had, however, been a few complaints of rolling on the GCR main line.

In post-war days the design came under a cloud following two derailments on poor track. The Gresley swing link pony truck was replaced by a spring controlled truck giving more side control and this, coupled with a gradual improvement of the road, removed much of the anxiety. For some years, though, it was normal practice to restrain the V2s somewhat and it is said that when a VIP was to travel over the GCR main line the Motive Power Superintendent, the late L. P. Parker, gave strict instructions to the locomotive inspector on the footplate that downhill speeds were to be restricted to 70 mph or under as the engine was a V2. In the mid-1950s, however, speeds of over 80 mph could be recorded on the GCR behind V2 class engines.

There were few detailed variations among the 184 engines in the class through the years. The first five engines had the earlier type of front valve spindle guide as used on the A3s; later engines had a modified pattern, as did the later A4s. No 813 had a stove-pipe chimney and a curious shovel-shaped deflector plate fitted in 1947

which it retained until its end in 1966. In their last days, when
cylinders needed replacement, the monobloc casting was replaced
be separate cast cylinders with outside steam pipes similar to those
of the A3s. Following the successful conversions to double blast of
the A3s and A4s the ER wished to make similar experiments with
some V2s, but by then steam was on its way out and the BTC was
reluctant to sanction any more expenditure on a type of motive
power with a poor life expectancy. It was, however, permitted for
Nos 60817 and 60963 to be fitted with the simple plain double
blastpipe as used on the "Royal Scots" and on some BR engines.
The steaming of these engines proved to be little better than that of
the single blast engines. Later, conversion was sanctioned for five
engines to the Kylchap arrangement and these represented the final
form of the V2. The conversion came late but there were a few
significant performances. The engines concerned were Nos 60858/
902/3 with the original cylinders and Nos 60862/81 with the separate
cylinder castings.

When the engines were being built at Doncaster a visiting party
was told that they were to be black, so the appearance of 4771 in
apple green was a pleasant surprise. The green was applied to all
engines built at Darlington up to 4894, after which wartime black
took over. The Doncaster-built engines 3655–7 were painted green
when built. Doncaster engines had their cylinder casings black but
Darlington painted them green. In post-war days only No 4854
reverted to the apple green. The rest remained black with straw Gill
Sans numbering. This was followed in BR days by the LNWR-type
lined black livery, at first with British Railways on the tender and
later with the insignia. Finally the class all received BR Brunswick
green. They were quite good-looking engines, but it is sad to record
that they were often in a pitiable state of grime which detracted
from their appearance. It was a long and varied road from the debut
of No 4771 *Green Arrow* at Doncaster in 1936 to its present state of
preservation but so far without a permanent home. The performances
recorded during this chequered existence were a most varied
selection.

CHAPTER NINE

"Green Arrow" Performance in Peace and War

The design of the "Green Arrow" class 2-6-2s gave promise of good running. There were no risky design features in the thermodynamic field and the record of the K3 class Moguls and the *Cock o' the North* class engines gave no fears about unsafe riding at high speeds. Perhaps if more LNER enthusiasts had ridden on the K3s when they reached their 80 mph maxima between Leeds and Doncaster or between Leicester and Nottingham then a different viewpoint would have prevailed. In 1936 the GNR main line had been brought up to a very high standard of maintenance for the high-speed streamliners and it was in any case one of Britain's straightest main lines. It was perhaps not realised at first quite how fast the new mixed traffic 2-6-2s would have to run in the next few years. There were, after all, a large number of Pacific type express engines on the East Coast main line and the original intention was to employ the 2-6-2s mainly on the fast fitted freight trains up till then handled by the K3 2-6-0s. The name *Green Arrow* was an indication of the main role proposed for the new engines. The first engine of the class, No 4771, was allocated to Kings Cross and it was frequently used on the famous 3.40 pm down "Scotch Goods". At busy periods there were still quite a lot of main-line specials which were worked by Atlantics or K3s, so it was confidently expected that it would not be long before the new 2-6-2s would be seen on expresses.

In the summer holiday season of 1936 all expectations were soon fulfilled and No 4771 was seen on express passenger trains at the weekends. That unfailing observer of all things of interest on the GNR main line, R. A. H. Weight, was soon able to report the working of a 600 ton load by 4771 on the 10.53 pm relief Newcastle and Sunderland express. The first detailed log was published by Cecil J. Allen in April 1936, when a run by 4771 on the 1.5 pm relief to the 1.20 pm "Scotsman" was described. It was confidently expected that an engine with 6 ft 2 in wheels would run quickly uphill and moderately downhill. There was reason for this expect-ation, for the initial trial of *Cock o' the North* had displayed just that characteristic, while, in 1920, one of the first K3 Moguls had run from Kings Cross to Peterborough in even time without exceeding 65 mph. These runs were, however, special test runs with the drivers working under strict instructions. The run on the 1.5 pm was a run in ordinary service conditions, where the driver was running the engine in the way he found most suitable for the job. The details of this first published run caused some surprise at first, but in the light of subsequent happenings, even up to the published test report of the 1950s, the indications of this first published performance were significant.

The run was the exact opposite of what was expected as the load of 427 tons tare, 455 tons full, was taken slowly out of Kings Cross and up to Potters Bar. This may have meant an engine that was a shy steamer, but there is also the possibility that the driver knew that he had tight margins ahead and this idea is supported by the fact that a signal check was suffered at Potters Bar. Whatever the reason the train passed Hatfield 4½ min behind time in 31 min 20 sec, but then followed a spell of fast running downhill and on the level which was comparable with the high contemporary standards of the Pacifics. The average from Hatfield to Fletton, 57.3 miles was 71.9 mph, from Stevenage to Huntingdon, 30.3 miles, was 76.5 mph and the maximum at Three Counties was 86.5 mph. This resulted in the recovery of all the lost time and Peterborough was passed 1 min early.

It was expected that the 2-6-2 would accelerate quickly from the Peterborough slack, but the actual recovery was very slow and speed was only 51 mph at Essendine, after which the engine was opened out sufficiently to maintain speeds of from 46 to 48 mph up to Stoke Box, but arrival in Grantham was 40 sec late. There is no way of knowing for certain, after so many years, just why the 2-6-2 was driven in this way; it may have been that the engine was shy for steam and for that reason it was taken slowly up the banks and allowed to find its own pace downhill taking advantage of the excellent road. It was, however, fully in the GNR tradition to run easily uphill and quickly downhill on the easily timed trains on the GNR main line. This had been the normal way of driving the Atlantics and it may have been the only way of keeping time with the saturated engines, but the tradition continued with the superheated Atlantics and the Pacifics. It was a wise method of driving trains on such a good road; the risks involved in running downhill at 85–90

mph were minimal, on such a straight route there was little dis-
comfort for passengers and there is little doubt that overall coal
consumption was reduced. When the French raised the maximum
speed limit on the Region du Nord from 74.5 to 81 mph coal consumption was reduced by allowing the very powerful Collin and
Chapelon Pacifics to ascend the banks without flogging while
reaching 80 mph downhill with the greatest ease. There is little
doubt that the driver of No 4771 would have tackled the 118 min
schedule of the 1.5 pm down in a similar way had he been given a
Pacific.

There were trains on the GNR main line, especially after 1935,
which needed hard running uphill and down and the most exciting
assignment ever to fall to the lot of a V2 was when No 4789 had to
replace an A4 at the last minute when a minor fault had been
discovered after the engine was attached to the down "West Riding
Limited" streamliner at Kings Cross. It is to be regretted that no
detailed log exists of the V2 performance, but R. A. H. Weight, a
most expert observer of GNR running, estimated that the engine
only lost 4 min on the very exacting schedule of this train. The late
start had put the train out of its path and some signal delays were
inevitable, but a schedule of 163 min to Leeds on which the engine
had dropped 4 min would still leave a net time of 167 min and a net
start to stop average of 66.7 mph for the 185.7 miles. Running of this
nature could not have been accomplished without some vigorous
uphill work as well as fast descents. The long 1 in 200 banks would
almost certainly have been topped at around 70 mph, while well
sustained speeds in the region of 90 mph would be needed on the
level and downhill sections. The eight-coach set weighed 275 tons
tare, 290 tons gross. This was, with little doubt, the fastest run ever
made by a mixed traffic engine in Britain up to that time. Had the
aim of the V2 design been to provide a fast goods engine, then it
might have been claimed, with some justice, by GWR supporters
that the 4700 class 2-8-0 was a cheaper and equally effective design,
but not even the most extreme GWR fanatic could reasonably have
claimed that a 4700 class 2-8-0 could have timed the "Bristolian".
The LNER 2-6-2 had taken the mixed traffic conception into a new
dimension. A V2 had also taken the place of a failed A4 on the down
"Coronation" from York northwards. No details are available as to
how this engine performed but the "Coronation" north of York
was more easily timed than the "West Riding Limited" between
Kings Cross and Leeds.

In the summer of 1939 the "Yorkshire Pullman" was run on several occasions by V2 class engines from Doncaster shed. This train had a 60 mph booking between Doncaster and Kings Cross and those who had seen the V2s running well up to time had their curiosity aroused. This curiosity was satisfied by Cecil J. Allen in his article in the December 1939 *Railway Magazine*. The first run featured Driver Sherriff of Doncaster with No 4817 and a load of 9 Pullmans weighing 362 tons tare, 380 tons full. The train made a moderate start from Doncaster as one of the injectors was giving trouble. Trouble of this kind was by no means unknown on Gresley engines as no change in pipe size had been made since the original No 1470 of 1922 and it was only in the final days of thes A4s that larger bore piping brought some improvement. (In fairness it must be added that the LMS was far from being free of similar trouble.) After Retford, No 4817 had recovered and some fine work followed with 54 at Markham, 83½ at Carlton and a minimum of 53 mph at Peascliffe until a signal check slowed the Pullman before Grantham, after which speed recovered to 53 mph and was sustained at 50 mph up to Stoke Box. Then followed a descent to Werrington well up to Pacific standards; the 17.6 miles from Corby to Werrington were reeled off at an average of 86.2 mph and the 7.4 miles from Bytham to Tallington at 90.2 mph with a maximum of 93 mph. There had been a gain of 3¾ min between Grantham and Peterborough alone. After Peterborough the good work continued despite a signal check at Holme. The journey was completed in 151 min 44 sec, 3¼ min under schedule and in a net time of 147½ min for the 156 miles. With a normal start from Doncaster another minute could have been gained.

The second run, by No 4792, had a heavier load of 395 tons tare and 415 tons gross and was less spectacular. Time was kept quite comfortably with lower speeds downhill, but the recovery from 50 mph at Hitchin to 53 mph at Stevenage Summit needed more hp than anything developed by 4817. A run by an A4 which was 5 min faster than either of the V2s was included in the same table of runs. The downhill speed of 93 mph created great enthusiasm, but this was reduced somewhat in 1946 when a run which included a maximum speed of 92 mph by an LMS Black Five was published by Cecil J. Allen. The LMS run was between Luton and Bedford with a load of 400 tons and so was of equal merit. The V2s had not pro- duced any very remarkable uphill speeds, though they certainly did everything that the timetable required. The same article by Cecil J.

Allen included details of a run also by Driver Sherriff on the "York-shire Pullman", where the booked A3 had to be replaced at Grantham by Atlantic No 4401. In this case the time from Hunting-don to Hitchin, with 380 tons, was less than that of either of the V2s only slightly more heavily loaded and the minimum speed at Stevenage Summit was only slightly slower. The V2s were clearly not needing to be extended to anything like their maximum capacity to gain slightly on the booking of one of the crack ordinary GN main line expresses. It is to be regretted that no details survive of the uphill work of the V2 on the much more difficult streamlined "West Riding Limited".

There was one heavily loaded train on the GN main line that required a much greater power output than the general average and that was the "Flying Scotsman", with its exceptionally heavy stock introduced in 1938. There appears to be no record of a V2 on this job, but it was reported that a V2 brought a 490 ton "Junior Scotsman" into Kings Cross on time having made an even time run up from Grantham. This performance was destined to be repeated after the war several times. The fast goods trains for which the engines were intended were normally beyond the reach of recorders but it was apparent to the lineside observer that the engines were completely masters of their work on the fast fitted freights. The LNER in those days regarded the down "Scotch Goods" in particular with almost the same favour as the "Flying Scotsman" or the streamlined trains. For a period No 4771 *Green Arrow* was to be seen on this job, turned out in immaculate fashion by Kings Cross shed.

There was a large allocation of V2 class engines to the NER section and they took over much of the work previously performed by Atlantics either alone or in pairs. They were well received in Scotland and a Canadian locomotive engineer, with worldwide experience, praised the riding qualities of No 4793 over the Edin-burgh–Aberdeen main line, which was a course likely to throw into sharp relief any deficiency in stability.

The V2s visited the GCR first on specials and a picture of No 4773 passing Sudbury Hill on a cup final special from Sunderland to Wembley Hill was published in July, 1937. Later they appeared on the night trains to Newcastle and on the Penzance–Aberdeen. They were, in general, well received and they were clearly masters of their work although, like other Gresley three-cylinder engines with limited cut off in full gear, they could be awkward when faced with a baulked start on a steep gradient. A retired GCR locomotive inspector tells of the difficulty experienced in getting away from an emergency stop at Rickmansworth following the pulling of the communication cord. Several set backs were needed before the 13 coach train could be got going again. There were also complaints of rolling on the descent from Woodhead and between Wendover and Aylesbury.

Leicester received Nos 4830 and 4845 and these were intended mainly for the Marylebone–Newcastle night trains, but in practice they soon found their way on to the London trains including the famous 6.20 pm from Marylebone. In pre-war days Leicester maintenance was remarkably good, as is proved by their excellent record with the Atlantics and "Sandringhams", and they did very good work with the minimum of trouble on their V2s in 1939. They had not the same enthusiasm for V2s which came from other sections, especially from the NER.

It was with V2 No 4830 that Driver Tetlow of Leicester achieved what must have been the fastest run on GCR metals ever to appear in print. The 6.20 pm had a light load of seven bogies weighing 242 tons tare, 255 tons full, and the first few miles brought many delays, with the result that the 6.20 was 8 min late at High Wycombe, but after Princes Risborough a clear road was obtained and the 2-6-2 made good use of it. A maximum speed of $87\frac{1}{2}$ mph was reached at Haddenham and between Ashendon and Grendon Junction speed was held at between 78 and $83\frac{1}{2}$ mph. After a minimum of 75 mph at Calvert 80 mph was again touched in the dip before the 1 in 176, up which speed fell to 70 mph before shutting off steam for Finmere. Speed had averaged 80.5 mph for 19.5 miles. The train left Finmere in a raging thunderstorm and attained $65\frac{1}{2}$ in the dip before Brackley, after which it fell to 59 mph on the 1 in 176 and was up to $78\frac{1}{2}$ mph before the Woodford stop. The start to stop run of 14.6 miles of undulating road with a rising tendency had been completed in 16 min 3 sec. The lateness had now been reduced to $3\frac{1}{2}$ min, but ahead lay an even time booking of 34 min for the 34 miles to Leicester. The arrival in Leicester was half a minute early and the way in which this was done is best shown in tabular form:

Distance		Min	sec	Speeds
				mph
0.0	Woodford	00	00	
2.1	Charwelton	4	42	
6.1	Staverton Road	8	04	81
9.4	Braunston	11	19	90

14.1	Rugby	13	43	76
17.7	Shawell Box	16	32	83/65½
20.9	Lutterworth	19	18	65½
24.8	Ashby Magna	22	36	88
29.3	Whetstone	25	51	
33.0	Leicester Goods Junct	28	25	
34.0	Leicester	30	09	

The average speed from Staverton Road to Leicester Goods Junction was 79.3 mph for 26.9 miles and a total of 46½ miles of the journey had been completed at an average of 80 mph. The engine had gained 9 min on the very fast schedule, but the load of 255 tons was, of course, light for so large an engine. The details of this GCR run, however, made it easily possible to understand why No 4789 a year earlier had done so well on the "West Riding Limited" streamliner on the GN main line, which was more suitable for very high speeds.

When these details were first published in December 1939 the nation was well into the period of "phoney war" and it was in wartime that the V2s rose to high esteem, while performing work of a very different character. In their relatively short period of pre-war peacetime service they had, in general, fulfilled expectations. The LNER had in its hand the tools for making a telling blow at long-distance road competition by accelerated fitted freight services while less reliance had to be placed on aging Atlantics, sometimes in pairs, and on K3s flogged along at speeds which were distinctly uncomfortable for their crews. Almost everyone was satisfied except the amateur lineside photographers who enjoyed getting two for the price of one when an Atlantic with a pilot came into their viewfinders.

The war brought the V2s into what many people consider to be the most useful phase of their lives. The fast fitted freight services disappeared, but the wartime express passenger trains resembled the loads and speeds of the pre-war freights. Under these conditions Pacifics and V2s shared the work and both classes also put in a lot of time on unfitted goods trains. It has been claimed that the V2s were "the engines which won the war", but in fairness it must be said that the Pacifics did just as well, while the LMS supporters made a similar claim for their Black Fives. Politically the V2s had an important advantage. It had been decreed that no "express" engines were to be built for the duration, but by virtue of their 6 ft 2 in wheels, the construction of V2s continued until 1944 and they were of great value to the company and the nation. They were terribly abused in the latter part of the war, but earlier they ran well with vast loads. The fact that they were big with ample reserve power told against them, as their maintenance was neglected in a way that might well have brought a smaller engine to a stop.

One of the heaviest locomotive hauled passenger trains ever to run in Britain was the 26 coach load of 764 tons tare, 860 tons gross, hauled by No 4800 from Peterborough to Kings Cross, 76.4 miles, in 102 min. A faster time of 96 min was made by *Persimmon* and indeed some of the best running with the very heavy wartime loads was to the credit of the earlier Pacifics with 180 lb boiler pressure. A good V2 performance with a heavy wartime load was recorded by R. A. H. Weight and F. C. Witt when No 4886 brought a 20 coach load of 700 gross tons from Newcastle to York, 80.2 miles, in 95 min. Speed was sustained at over 60 mph for many level miles between Darlington and York, which stretch was covered in 46 min pass to stop. This was followed by a time of 98 min net from York to Grantham. The V2 had gained $11\frac{1}{4}$ min on the easy wartime schedule. No 4884 took a 700 ton train from Doncaster to Peterborough, 76.6 miles, in 89 min 35 sec despite easy downhill running, while a Grantham doctor timed No 4786, with Grantham driver J. W. Handley and 690 tons, from his home town to Kings Cross in 121 min 20 sec for the 105.5 miles. The finest sectional time was $27\frac{1}{2}$ min for the 27, generally rising, miles from Huntingdon to Hitchin.

As the war continued maintenance became an increasing problem and during the final two years of war a maximum of 18 bogies was only rarely exceeded. Good work, however, sometimes was recorded, as when one of the writers timed No 4785 at the head of an 18 coach load of 630 tons gross which was brought from Kings Cross to Grantham in 125 min 18 sec or in 123 min net. An excellent start for such a load was made when Finsbury Park was passed in 7 min 38 sec and Potters Bar in 23 min 48 sec. The 15.3 miles from Tallington to Stoke Summit took 17 min 30 sec with a time of 3 min 50 sec for the final 3 miles of 1 in 178. No 4785 was apparently a good engine at that time, as a run timed by H. J. J. Griffith was published by Cecil J. Allen in 1944, when a 620 ton load was taken past Finsbury Park in 8 min 5 sec, but harder work on the 1 in 200 put the second run 25 sec ahead of the first at Potters Bar. The second run was faster from Hitchin to Huntingdon, but a few seconds slower from Huntingdon to mp 62.

All wartime running was not at the same level and shortly after the 123 min from Kings Cross to Grantham with 630 tons the same recorder had the misery of timing a V2 with a 550 ton load from Grantham to Stoke Box in $17\frac{1}{2}$ min, while later in the same journey an unchecked run from Peterborough to Kings Cross took two solid hours. There were thoughts that all was far from well with the Gresley engines, but the next weekend brought a run by the Thompson "improvement" No 3697 which took 34 min to drag a 590 ton load past Potters Bar and $31\frac{1}{2}$ min were needed from Tallington to Stoke. The return journey brought an excellent run by *Seagull*, so the only fair conclusion was that it was not easy to operate a railway in wartime. No mention of the V2 war record would be complete without some reference to Driver Skerritt of Grantham, who took over an up express in an emergency and kept sectional time from Retford to Grantham with No 4851 tender-first. When peace finally came the V2s had certainly done their bit and more.

CHAPTER TEN

Post-War V2 Performance

At the close of World War II the LNER made a courageous but, as it proved, premature, return towards faster running on the GNR main line. The maximum loads were reduced from the wartime 18 bogies or over so that a 15 coach formation was rarely exceeded, but the timings were tightened up. Schedules of 117 and 120 min reappeared as the up and down times between Grantham and Kings Cross. Such timings resembled those of the 500 ton East Coast expresses in the years leading up to the accelerations of 1932, but the task in 1945/6 was much more difficult owing to more speed restrictions, a general limitation on downhill maximum speeds and the poor mechanical condition of many of the engines. Fuel also was generally of poor quality, with the result that timekeeping was poor, while locomotive failures were far too frequent. There had to be some decline from these hopeful schedules when railway travelling reached a miserably low standard during the big snows of 1947. Speeds gradually began to improve on a sounder foundation during the 1950s.

In 1945/6 Pacifics and V2s continued to be pooled in the wartime manner and they tackled the main-line trains on a basis of equality with no apparent advantage to either type. The one thing that did emerge from travelling and lineside observation during the first few years of peace was that the best engines on the line were the four Kylchap double blast A4s, which could usually be relied on to give a better than average performance. The W1 No 10000 also seemed well on top of its work. During weeks in the autumn of 1945 leading up to the demobilisation of one of the writers, there was frequent indulgence in the serviceman's practice of the "crafty weekend" and this led to regular journeys between Grantham and Kings Cross. The down train was usually a Saturday relief to the afternoon "Scotsman" and this usually loaded to 12 bogies behind a V2. Occasionally speed would rise to 75 mph at Three Counties and in the rare event of a clear run Peterborough would be reached in just over or under 85 min. From the Peterborough start Grantham was usually reached in 37–40 min with times of 20–21 min from Tallington to the Summit. This was rather uninspiring running, but then suddenly one Saturday, for no apparent reason, a good V2 ran the 29.1 miles to Grantham in $31\frac{1}{2}$ min start to stop with a time of $15\frac{1}{2}$ min from Tallington to the Summit. Such running was, of course, in no way sensational as *Seagull* had climbed the bank just as quickly, earlier in the war, with 660 tons, but it was a cheerful experience against a generally gloomy contemporary background.

In 1946 the V2 design was criticised following two derailments on poor track. On good track the engines had given few bad moments, but the derailments of 1946 caused a serious look to be taken at the two-wheeled leading truck. As the new design with spring-loaded side control came into general use and as track returned to something nearer to its pre-war standard the V2s began occasionally to show something of their old energy. In September 1950 Cecil J. Allen was able to publish a run with V2 No 60889 at the head of a 14 coach load of 510 tons gross. There was some trouble with priming in the early stages and Potters Bar, 12.7 miles from Kings Cross, was passed in 13 sec over the 20 min, which used to be regarded as the criterion for a good 8 footer with over 200 tons. The remainder of the journey to Peterborough was typical of a Gresley engine at its best, making full use of the excellent racing ground. The net average speed for 31 miles from Knebworth to Offord was 76.5 mph and the maximum, at Three Counties, was 84 mph but even better was 80 mph on little easier than level track at Tempsford. The run was timed by G. W. Carpenter and the driver, who had used full regulator and relatively short cut offs for most of the fast running, was a second link man making his first but by no means his last appearance in print. His name was W. Hoole of Kings Cross shed.

The early 1950s were, however, far from being happy years on the East Coast route and for every brilliant run there were many which were well below the standard to be expected of a large Pacific or 2-6-2 on a relatively easy road. There were many criticisms in the daily press of bad timekeeping and frequent engine failures. In the autumn of 1951 drastic changes were made in order to improve matters. The ruling spirit behind the changes was the late L. P. Parker, the Motive Power Superintendent, who took the bold step of introducing engine changing of far greater frequency and allowing for a closer association between engines and men at each depot. Grantham shed undertook a larger number of main-line workings and the reputation of Kings Cross shed rose as certain selected engines and crews ran with greater certainty. The wartime pooling of engines had outlived its useful life and it no longer allowed for the efficient running of faster main-line expresses. In general the V2s were left outside the selection of engines specially well looked after for the expresses, but Kings Cross had always paid great attention to the fitted freights and some of the Kings Cross stud of V2s were well cared for and performed well on the fast freights, while even some of the begrimed inhabitants of New England shed were not always as bad as they looked.

In 1953 Cecil J. Allen joined the up "White Rose" at Grantham without knowing which type of engine was at the head of the 450 ton train. The "White Rose" ran briskly up to Kings Cross with times of 30¾ min Grantham–Peterborough and 77 min net on to Kings Cross. As the recorder made his way to the front he fully expected to find a top link A1 or A4 class Pacific, but the train had been headed by a grimy V2 No 60950, reputedly one of New England's best.

In the mid 1950s the V2s could spring surprises even on that expert batch of East Coast enthusiasts who did so much recording and platform end observation. They would see off a friend behind a clean V2 of immaculate reputation, only to learn later of a sorry tale of time lost, but on other occasions they would predict that the dirty old warrior, overdue for shops, at the head of a smartly timed train could never measure up to the job, only to appear as false prophets when a good run was recorded. In the previous chapter there was a pre-war run from Grantham to Kings Cross in even time with 490 tons; on several occasions runs of comparable merit were recorded in the 1950s. On one such occasion P. J. Coster was travelling on the up relief to the "Heart of Midlothian" with a 13 coach load of 490 tons. At Grantham V2 No 60943 of Kings Cross, with a Grantham crew, took over. The engine had run a high mileage and nothing in the way of fast running was expected. As they churned their way up to Stoke the irregular beat did nothing to inspire confidence. However, Stoke Box was passed at 46 mph in the surprisingly good time, for an engine starting cold at Grantham, of 10 min 6 sec, while an average speed of 90.3 mph between mps 93 and 83 with a maximum of 93 mph at Essendine was even better. Werrington was passed in 25 min 43 sec from Grantham and after signal delays. Peterborough was passed, on the excursion road, in 31 min 25 sec. There was no holding engine and crew as they got up to 75 mph at Connington and topped Ripton Bank at 61 mph, were checked to 23 mph at Paxton, but recovered to 74 at Tempsford, finally clearing

Stevenage at 58 mph. The net time from Grantham to Kings Cross was at most 107 min. At least 1 min more should be added to post-war times to allow for the more restricted speeds on the descent from Potters Bar as compared with the higher speeds which were normal before 1939. On another occasion P. J. Coster saw the up "Flying Scotsman" arrive at Kings Cross one afternoon in 1955 with the redoubtable Bill Hoole in charge of No 60855, newly ex-Plant, instead of the expected A4 No 60007. If the train had left Grantham on time the 105.5 miles had been covered in 106 min. The load was 515 tons. At least one more 106 min run with 500 tons has been recorded and there may have been other occasions which were never timed.

Later in the 1950s more through workings from Kings Cross to Newcastle were introduced and in May, 1958 the down "Flying Scotsman" set off for Newcastle behind A1 No 60157 with Bill Hoole at the regulator, Fireman Pettinghall at the shovel and with Norman Harvey, an experienced recorder, on board with his stop watch. The A1 had to be replaced at Peterborough by V2 No 60869, but the substitute engine brought the 405 ton train into Newcastle, 191.9 miles from Peterborough, in 200½ min or 190½ min net. While Driver Hoole was taking the measure of his new engine Stoke bank was climbed at the creditable, but by no means outstanding, minimum speed of 58 mph. The maximum speed of the run was 84 mph at Claypole, while 75 mph northbound through Thirsk was again good but not exceptional. Perhaps the best piece of hill climbing came towards the end of the run, after three hours of hard steaming, when 60869 increased speed up 1 in 203 past Bradbury to 60 mph. The full story of this run and of another occasion when a run-down V2 had to take the "Tees Tyne Pullman" up from York, is told in the excellent book *Bill Hoole, Engineman Extraordinary* by P. W. B. Semmens (Ian Allan, 1965). There were other occasions when V2s did well in similar emergencies, but it must be said that other substitutions were less successful.

On the NER section the V2s showed their ability to run well on the level racing ground across the Plain of York. Speeds of up to 85 mph and well sustained averages of 80 mph were run on a road little easier than level with loads of 400 tons and such running compared well with anything recorded by contemporary Class 7 engines on other lines. In Scotland the V2s were popular and many retired drivers consider them to have been the most generally useful machines ever to have run on the Edinburgh–Aberdeen section, but the published records contain no V2 runs which could not equally well have been performed by the A3s. In fact it can be said that nowhere is there any evidence that the 6 ft 2 in driving wheels gave the engines any advantage uphill over the Pacifics with 6 ft 8 in wheels. Although there are some individual feats of hill climbing to the credit of the Gresley Pacifics and 2-6-2s, generally speaking they were happier at fast running on a good road than in hard slow speed slogging up very steep gradients. In 1954 Cecil J. Allen described two runs, timed by Ronald Nelson, a most experienced recorder, between Aberdeen and Montrose. On the first run V2 No 60971 reached 92½ mph downhill on crossing the North Esk at Craigo while No 60958 reached 90 mph at the same spot, in both cases with loads of around 400 tons. On falling grades the attainment of such speeds was not difficult but it is significant that there was full confidence to let the engines run on curving track—a compliment to the redesigned leading truck.

Some of the best work ever performed by the V2s took place on the GCR and went unrecorded. They never seemed to do anything remarkable for their size on the Sheffield–Manchester section and the sure-footed Robinson 4-6-0 mixed traffic engines got away with more certainty from locations such as Guide Bridge. The V2s were happier when the bank could be charged at speed and in 1956/58 the down "Newspaper" had a sectional booking of 19 min for the 18.5 miles from Calvert to Culworth Junction; with a load of 400 tons tare, mostly newspaper vans stacked to the roof with newsprint, the gross load would be exceptionally heavy. This needed 35 per cent cut off and a noise in the small hours which might have caused complaint had the line run through more densely populated country. A run-down engine could fail to keep time and give anxiety about water level. On some of the best runs, when a minute or so was cut from the pass to pass timing, the edbhp would rise to the 1600 mark.

In November 1946 test running took place on the NER section between Newcastle and Leeds and Newcastle and Edinburgh. The aim was to test the new Thompson Class A2/3 Pacific No 500 *Edward Thompson* against a V2 and the V2 selected was the Haymarket favourite No. 959. Undue significance should not be attached to these tests as much more can be learned from the 1953 tests on the Swindon Plant. The conclusions of the 1946 tests were predictable: the A2/3 had the greater reserve of power, which was hardly surprising in view of the greater size of the Pacific. The whole Kylchap blast pipe and chimney combination was found to be superior to the

V2s on Named Expresses

Top: V2 No 60983 near Abbotts Ripton with the up *Flying Scotsman* in July 1952.

[*Eric Treacy*

Above: The up *Scarborough Flier* heads southwards from Grantham behind V2 No 60814 on 8-8-59.   [*T. Boustead*

The Grantham Area

Opposite page:

Top: V2 No 60909 in Saltersford Cutting with an up fitted freight, June 1952.   *[J. F. Clay*

Centre: V2 No 60935 entering the Saltersford Cutting with a down loose coupled freight, June 1952.   *[J. F. Clay*

Bottom: V2 No 60809 *The Snapper* at Grantham on August 1961.   *[K. R. Pirt*

The GCR Main Line

Top: V2 No 60879 entering Nottingham Victoria on the up *Master Cutler*.
     [T. G. Hepburn

Above: V2 No 60842 passing Aylestone on an up Marylebone express 1959.
     [D. W. Webb

The GN/GE Joint Line

Top: V2 No 60907 on a Doncaster March freight leaving Lincoln August 10th, 1950.
[J. F. Henton

Above: V2 No 60803 leaving Lincoln on joint line express.
[R. E. Vincent

SR Emergency

Top: V2 No 60917 on SR West of England express about to leave Waterloo, in June 1953.   *[W. J. Reynolds*

Above: V2 No 60896 on down *Bournemouth Belle* on July 6th, 1953.   *[Modern Transport*

WR Test Running

Above: V2 No 60845 on Stoke Gifford–Reading controlled road test with a 20 coach load. The speed had just been deliberately reduced by brakes to 15–20mph for test purposes after passing through Badminton station. *[P. M. Alexander*

V2s in Scotland

Opposite page

Top: V2 No 60813 with smoke deflecting device, at Beattock Summit with down freight. *[T. G. Hepburn*

Bottom: V2 No 60972 leaving Stonehaven. *[T. G. Hepburn*

V2s in Scotland

Opposite page:

Top: V2 No 60888 on fish train passing North Queensferry.   *[J. Robertson*

Bottom: Stranger on the West Coast line. V2 No 60838 heads the morning Perth–Euston train through the Clyde Valley between Lamington and Wandel Mill in early March 1961.   *[Derek Cross*

Above: The afternoon up *Postal* passing Hilt on Junction, Perth behind ex works V2 No 60919 on 21st August 1963.   *[S. C. Crook.*

Top: V2 No 60891 taking the Waverley Route at Portobello with the up *Waverley* express.
[Eric Treacy

Into the 1960s

Above: V2 No 60862 with outside steam pipes and double chimney leaving Grantham on a down relief Newcastle express on 1-5-62.
[J. F. Henton

Top: V2 No 60805 passing New Basford on a down fitted freight on 10-6-63
[T. Boustead

Above: V2 No 60963 entering Leicester London Road station on a Newcastle to Margate special on 4-5-65. *[G. Morgan*

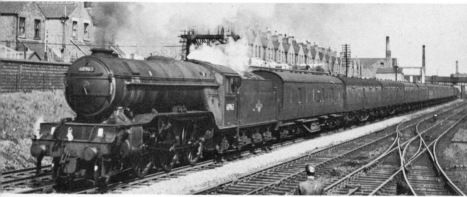

Top: V2 No 60879 entering Rushcliffe Halt on a Nottingham–Leicester stopping train.
[T. G. Hepburn

Centre: The 11.15am Nottingham Victoria–Marylebone Parcels train passing Leicester South Goods Box behind V2 No 60963 (50A) with double chimney on April 18th, 1964.
[H. A. Gamble

The Final Years

V2 No. 60836 climbs towards Granthouse with the Altrinchamian Railway Society Waverley Special on 23-3-66. This was one of the last passenger workings by a V2. *[J. Lummas*

V2 No 60831, the last to remain in service in England, passing York on a freight train on Sept. 12th, 1966. *[P. N. Clay*

The preserved V2 No 4771 *Green Arrow* stored at Leicester MPD May 4th, 1969. *[H. A. Gamble*

Bottom left: V2 No 60871 hauling a dead BRCW Type 3 diesel through Grantham station, April 1962. *[J. F. Clay*

Above: The new V4 No 3401 *Bantam Cock* on trial on the GER section near Cambridge on a Norwich–Liverpool Street express loaded to over 450t tare.   *[E. R. Wethersett*

Gresley's Last Design

Opposite page:

Top: V4 No 3401 *Bantam Cock* as originally built in LNER green.   *[LPC*

Centre: *Bantam Cock* renumbered 61700 at Eastfield Shed Glasgow in BR black on March 17th, 1949.   *[J. F. Henton*

Bottom: No 3401 *Bantam Cock* near Creagan Mill on the West Highland section at the head of the 3.46pm Glasgow–Fort William April 1944.   *[C. Lawson Kerr*

The second V4 No 61701 on a northbound coal train near Dairsie Fife.

[W. J. V. Anderson

single blast of the V2. The V2 attained short bursts of 1600–1660 edbhp, while the A2/3 was about 200 hp better than this at the same points. The maximum dbhps of 1600 are of interest as they are so close to the figures obtained by modern resistance formulae for maximum efforts on the GCR down "Newspaper".

It must be said, with regret, that the average standard of V2 running was at a much lower level than that indicated by the above selection of best post-war runs. This was, of course, true of most classes of steam locomotive during the same period and the subjective nature of steam performance contributed to the disappearance of a machine second to none as a centre of interest. Although individual runs of great merit were recorded by V2 engines throughout the life of the class it must be said that in the post-war years there was much running at a lower standard than should have been the case with engines of their size. The situation was made worse by the fitting of the LMS type self-cleaning screens in the smokeboxes of some V2s. This completely spoilt the steaming of engines which were having enough to contend with from poor coal and poor maintenance. To cure this trouble No. 60845, a New England engine of doubtful reputation, was sent to the Swindon Test Plant.

During the 1930s Gresley had persistently advocated the building of a locomotive testing station in Britain as a matter of urgency and he was the prime mover behind the Rugby Plant. Unfortunately he did not live to see its completion and opening in 1948, but the first engine to give a ceremonial twirl to the rollers was the A4 bearing his name. Ironically no Gresley engine was ever given the full treatment at Rugby and apart from 2001's visit to Vitry, the only one which received full dress trials was the V2 at Swindon. The engine was tested first as received with the self-cleaning plates in position and the steaming rate was a very modest 14000 lb/hr. This figure horrified Gresley enthusiasts, who wondered how so bad an engine could have run at all. In the 1928 trials of Pacifics Nos 4473 and 2544 between Doncaster and Kings Cross the evaporation rates varied between 14000 and 18000. The 1928 schedules were not as exacting as some of those run by the Pacifics in the 1935–1939 period, but they were harder than the average job given to a V2 in the 1950s. This initial test house figure, however, explained why the occasional disappointing run was not unknown in regular everyday service. Relatively small alterations to the blastpipe and chimney sufficed to more than double the steaming capacity and it was in this final condition that the full-dress trials were conducted.

The entire series of V2 trials was made with the Blidworth coal which was considered to be typical of the quality of coal usually given to a mixed traffic engine. Although we do not know for certain the test figures for a pre-war V2 with good quality coal, it may be a fair approximation to suggest that a pre-war engine with Grade 1 coal and no self-cleaning plates would have given figures very similar to those of the engine modified at Swindon using the Blidworth coal. The tests showed that the V2 gave a rather poor dbhp curve in the lower speed ranges. This appears to have been due to the unequal effort from the inside cylinder, resulting from the deficiencies of the 2 and 1 gear, and to a fairly high locomotive resitance. Some of the published indicator diagrams were not complimentary to the conjugate motion and instead of the expected diagrams some very weird shapes were traced. This was with a low mileage engine, admittedly not one with a high reputation, but one which had been, officially, at least restored to test condition. The question has, however, to be asked; if Gresley engines were really always as bad as this engine how was it that so many of the British speed records, both maximum and sustained, remain to the credit of Gresley engines? Clearly other arrangements of cylinders and valves had problems of their own and the innate elasticity of the steam locomotive allowed it to be built in many different forms and yet still give good results when properly handled.

Some indication of the value of the Gresley front end for high speed running emerged from the V2 trials, because at higher speeds and on early cut off working both drawbar and indicated hp performance was very good. In the table given on page 87 of *Locomotive Panorama* Vol 2 by E. S. Cox (Ian Allan, 1967) the figure for combined boiler and cylinder efficiency at minimum steam consumption rates is the highest of any engine in the British table. This optimum figure was recorded at an evaporation rate of 20000 lb/hr and at 1510 ihp, which meant that some very useful work could be performed with good economy. Boiler efficiency remained high throughout the range of steaming rates reaching 80 per cent, higher than any other comparable class, at around the 15000 lb/hr mark. At the maximum evaporation rate of 31000 lb/hr with a coal rate of 5670 lb/hr, the boiler efficiency fell to 59 per cent but even this figure was still comparable with other contemporary British designs. The V2 gave its best performances at the coal rates which corresponded to the running of a fast train under a light rein in regular service, but at lower speeds and at higher firing rates the coal/dbhp/hr figures

deteriorated. The conclusion is that the V2s were good high-speed
engines, but they were less suited to heavy slow-speed duties. The
findings of the test plant confirmed the conclusions which could be
drawn from their record on the road.

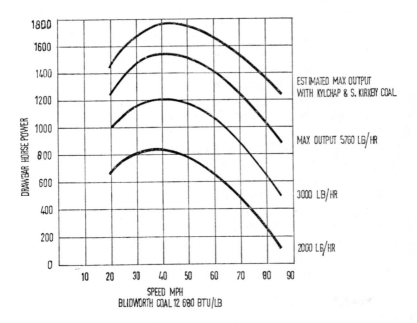

ESTIMATED MAX OUTPUT
WITH KYLCHAP & S. KIRKBY COAL

MAX OUTPUT 5760 LB/HR

3000 LB/HR

2000 LB/HR

SPEED MPH
BLIDWORTH COAL 12 680 BTU/LB

The figures on the lower three curves were those actually attained
but the upper curve has been estimated by adding the appropriate
percentage of additional hp for the use of high grade South Kirkby
coal and for the effect of the Kylchap double blast arrangements.
These percentages are those demonstrated by test results of other
engines. The upper figure has of course not been proved in actual
test conditions. If the details of the 68 mph climb to Stoke with 11
bogies on the "West Riding" are correct, figures similar to the above
curve were attained for possibly ten minutes. The pre-war single
blast engines on Grade 1 coal could, very possibly, have returned a
performance curve similar to the re-draughted engine on Blidworth
coal. Recorded performances support this conclusion.

The Swindon treatment did not spread quickly to the entire class,
but those engines which were modified were welcomed on the GCR.
They burnt more coal but did more work and they were considered

to be reliable machines which were less selective about fuel. Following the successful use of the Kylchap exhaust on A3s and A4s there were proposals to extend the double chimney to the V2s, but by then the sands were running out for steam and there was an official reluctance to spend more money on a type of motive power shortly to disappear. Two engines were fitted with the simple double blast-pipe as used on some LMS and BR standard engines, but these proved to be little better than the original single blast engines. Greater success was achieved by the five engines which were fitted with the full Kylchap arrangement as used on the A3s. It was with these engines that the full potential of the V2 was realised, but the conversion came too late for the improved engines to be fully exploited.

There were a number of substitutions at Peterborough in which Kylchap V2s relieved failed diesels and on a number of these occasions the replacements ran very well. More than once the Kylchap V2s ran the 76.4 miles in 74–75 min with loads of over 400 tons, but this was of course well within the capacity of a pre-war V2. On a trial trip with No 60881 shortly after conversion the inspector in charge said that had not the regulator been closed on the descent from Stoke the engine would have gone over the 100 mph mark. It would be interesting to know the exact figure attained before caution intervened.

Perhaps the greatest power output ever to have been made by a V2 at any period in the history of the class took place when the down "West Riding", 7.45 am from Kings Cross, had to give up its "Deltic" at Peterborough with a failing train-heating boiler. The Kylchap V2 which took over succeeded in passing Stoke Box at 68 mph with its 11 coach train. It is to be regretted that we have no detailed log, from which the edbhp could be calculated. In fact, it is ironical that full documentation eludes the two performances which must have been the best pre-war and post-war exploits of the V2 class; both took place under similar emergency conditions.

It is certainly true that the V2s gave better results at high speeds than in low speed slogging, but generally speaking they did very well on low-speed duties for the simple reason that they were big engines for the jobs they were called upon to do. They were roughly of the same size and weight as the P1 Mikados of 1925, but they were not required to work slow-speed freight trains even as heavy as those given to the 2-8-0s. In high-speed fitted freight service they remained good engines in post-war days as they had been before the war.

Some of the Kings Cross V2s were maintained in very good condition; they ran very well on the fitted freights and undertook a good deal of passenger work during the summer seasons.

Some of the best Kings Cross V2s ran over 8000 miles in a month during summer seasons, when some long-distance express mileage boosted the total. The New England V2s were generally considered to be in poor condition, but some were perhaps not as black as they appeared. Despite the good showing of the BR Britannia Pacifics and 2-10-0 9Fs in the test reports, former New England enginemen seem unanimous in their preference of a V2, even a run-down one, on both fitted freight and express duties over the Kings Cross–Peterborough section. The York V2s seem to have had a poor reputation, but they were popular in Scotland although the heavy banks, sharp curves and frequent stops soon seemed to cause motion and axleboxes to knock and glands to blow; but the alternative to a V2 was a Pacific which showed the same tendencies. The same troubles were present to a lesser extent among Pacifics and V2s used on the GCR. The long wheel-based Gresley engines were happier on the straight East Coast main line.

As time ran out for steam the V2s suffered along with the rest. As late as 1966, however, a V2 on a rail tour with 9 bogies ran at speeds of up to 82 mph with sustained running at 75 mph between Darlington and York. In their declining days on the GCR they were more popular than "Royal Scots" on the heavy night trains. The "Royal Scots" in their prime were capable of main-line work at least as good as anything recorded by a V2, but in the last extremity the big boiler counted. The design features which were praised when the engines were new meant less in old age. The wedge-fronted cab, which was so praised at first, meant very little when everything was black.

The V2 history was somewhat chequered, but it can be claimed with confidence that they were a success for the conditions for which they were built. Had peace continued they could have improved main-line freight services and countered road competition before it became consolidated. During the war they were a national asset, but in the difficult post-war world they were less successful. There was, perhaps, too much racehorse blood in the V2s for them to be successful hacks.

CHAPTER ELEVEN

"Bantam Cock":
Gresley's Last Design

The last two engines built by Gresley for the LNER, Nos 3401/2 of
Class V4, were probably his least-known and least appreciated class.
They were originally intended to be built in peacetime in 1939, but
construction was delayed by the start of war and it was not until
February 1941, only six weeks before Gresley's death, that No 3401
named *Bantam Cock* was actually finished, followed by 3402 in
March. It is understood that many more would have been built, but
that an order for ten more, for which cylinders were already cast,
was cancelled by Thompson.

Had peace continued the design might have proved very useful,
but it has been criticised as being too complicated and expensive for
wartime and for a post-war world in which steam locomotives faced
operating conditions little more favourable. It must be remembered
that the V4s were designed to provide a powerful mixed traffic
engine of very wide route availability. They were intended to travel
over 5000 route miles of the LNER, representing over 80 per cent of
the system, and as a result were classed RA4 under the route availability classification. They were unique in being such a powerful
engine with this lack of restriction—and such an engine was sorely
needed in the latter days of the LNER. It must be emphasised that
the LNER had, especially in East Anglia and Scotland, restrictions
more severe than those on other companies' lines. This requirement
was largely fulfilled in later years by the BR Class 4 75000 class
4-6-0, but these had much greater hammer blow than the V4s.

In order to provide this freedom Gresley had to keep axle loads
and hammer blow to a minimum, which had strong influence on the
selection of three-cylinder propulsion. Reciprocating masses were
reduced by the use of alloy steels, but the value of such practice
should be considered in the light of Dr Tuplin's comments in *Great
Northern Steam* (Ian Allan, 1971). Weight was further reduced by an
integrally forged piston and rod and there was further help from the
small cylinders of only 15 in diameter. The small cylinders were

possible because of the high boiler pressure of 250 lb/sq in, but boiler plate thickness had been kept down by using 2 per cent nickel steel plate. Gresley, in his later years, believed there was a thermodynamic advantage in the use of high pressure. The boiler had a pronounced taper reducing from 5 ft 4 in diameter at the firebox end to 4 ft 8 in diameter at the smokebox end. This reduced the weight of the boiler at the front end, but it also had the adverse effect of reducing the free area through the tubes and flues to the rather low figure of 12.8 per cent instead of a desirable 15 per cent for this size of grate. The actual value of the free gas area was slightly less than that of the BR 75000 and maximum steaming capacity could be expected to be about the same with the ability to burn rather poor coal due to the larger grate. In contrast the B1 figure of 16.2 per cent was excellent in this respect and possibly the V4 would have been a little tricky in sustained hard steaming on the main line.

The 2-6-2 wheel arrangement enabled a wide firebox of 28.5 sq ft grate area to be used with easy firing owing to the short throw. The trailing truck with its Cartazzi slides gave a good riding engine, which would doubtless have been more popular than the D49, the B17 and the K3. Piston valves were 7 in in diameter with a $1\frac{5}{8}$ in lap. This made for a free-running engine with ample steam passages to the small cylinders; if anything the ratio was more suitable for high-speed express work than for mixed traffic duties. Had the opportunity for a large class of V4s to establish a performance pattern ever materialised the type would doubtless have followed the trend of V2 performance in being best at high speeds on a good road.

The V4 has been compared unfavourably with Thompson's B1, which was deemed more suitable for wartime conditions, but it must be remembered that the B1 was an RA5 engine and in order to reduce hammer blow effects within this classification the amount of reciprocating balance had to be seriously reduced, causing the B1s to be rough riding and subject to fore-and-aft vibrations. The use of three cylinders on the V4s, besides reducing hammer blow, kept down piston thrusts and minimised the tendency to crack frames and loosen bolts, in contrast to a two-cylinder design of the same power and weight. Steam locomotive designers had to choose between various compromises and they could never find solutions of absolute merit to their various problems.

A well-known Scottish driver once described the V4s as running like a Rolls-Royce, but a former LNER engineer has said that they were "Rolls-Royces built to do a Ford car job". No 3402 was fitted with a welded steel firebox and thermic siphons when built and was probably regarded as a test bed for the possible future use of such features on larger engines taking shape on the Doncaster drawing boards. In practice, without properly controlled water treatment this proved troublesome and was replaced in 1945 by a copper firebox similar to that of 3401. As far as is known no spare boilers were built for the V4s and 3402 lay out of use minus boiler while this was being modified.

The high boiler pressure probably added to the deterioration from corrosion and this use of high pressure for a secondary engine has been a criticism of the design. It can be argued that a reduction of boiler pressure to 200 lb and an increase in cylinder size to $17\frac{1}{2}$ in $\times$ 26 in would have produced equivalent results, but the lighter boiler made possible by this would have reduced adhesion weight and increased the tendency to slip. If a lower pressure had been accepted, a larger boiler could have been provided within the same weight restrictions and possibly a modified GN Atlantic boiler with a shorter barrel could have been used. The larger cylinders would have provided a better cylinder efficiency for mixed traffic duties and better hill-climbing ability.

When new No 3401 was tested on the main line between Doncaster and Leeds on which 495 ton loads were successfully handled. It was then sent to the GE section, where it was tried over the majority of routes including the Southend line. It was used with great success on the Norwich expresses and proved to be most economical. On the round trip to Ipswich and back it was reported that only 30 cwts of coal were used despite a load of 12 bogies. No 3402 went straight to Scotland where the soft water was thought to have less corrosive effect on its steel firebox. It was joined by 3401 in early 1942 and after some trial running from Haymarket shed in the Perth and Fife areas, where it was found to equal a J38 0-6-0 in load haulage, they both settled at Eastfield in 1943, from where they were largely used on the West Highland line. Their comfortable cabs and good riding were much appreciated in winter but they do not seem to have been the equals of the K4s in hill-climbing; this was recognised by a load limit of 250 tons against 300 tons for the K4s. The V4s were faster on the easier stretches nearer Glasgow, where the smaller-wheeled K4s were rougher riding. The Haymarket men, used to Pacifics, found no difficulty in firing the V4s with a fairly thin fire, but men used to the deeper grates of the "Glens" and the K2s sometimes tended to fire too heavily and then the V4s ran short of steam. The

V4s, being a high-pressure engine, rapidly lost power with falling pressures on the banks. The alternative design with lower pressure and larger cylinders would have been superior to the actual engines. Like the K4s, the V4s could work right through to Mallaig in contrast to the B1s and Black Fives, which could be used to Fort William only.

Eventually, in 1954, they were transferred to Aberdeen, from where they were finally withdrawn as 61700 on 4/3/57 and 61701 on 26/11/57. They were used on fish trains and also on the GNS section, where they were more suited than the B1 class, which at first could not be used at all, and then only later with restrictions. It had been necessary on the GNS to retain the small-boilered B12/1s by reboilering with round top fireboxes owing to their small axle load. The V4s could replace the B12s on all but the Boat of Garton and Banff branches.

In 1946 Nos 3401/2 were renumbered 1700/1 and later became BR Nos 61700/1, the respective dates for this being 3401, 14/9/46 and 23/10/48; and 3402, 7/7/46 and 3/4/48.

As built they were painted in pre-war apple green with shaded lettering, but in about 1943 they were repainted in unlined black with NE lettering. No 1700 retained this until BR days, but 1701 received shaded LNER lettering while still black in 1946. It is believed that both reverted to apple green livery with unshaded lettering some time in 1947/8. Eventually they received BR lined livery, based on LNWR black, about 1950.

Little recorded performance is available, but in the *Railway Magazine* for July/August 1943 Cecil J. Allen published a run in which 3401 running from Perth to Edinburgh took 385 tons up the 1 in 70 to the Forth Bridge at a minimum speed of 23½ mph and later a maximum speed of 63 mph was attained at Turnhouse. Following the tradition of the V2s it can confidently be estimated that the V4 class, if multiplied, would have shown their maximum capacity on the GNR main line, where they might well have repeated the epic replacement efforts of the GN Atlantics with, most probably, a lower coal consumption. It could also be possible that future stars with the A4s might have done some very smart running with V4s on the Cambridge "Beer Trains".

The superiority of the B1 in maintenance may not have been the foregone conclusion which is the conviction of the majority. This would have been still more the case with the later type of middle big end. The V4 had an inherently lightly loaded big end—lower, for example, than the inside-cylindered engines, such as the B12 and D11 which were evidently considered satisfactory by Thompson. The design of crank and crank pin was identical with that of the V2s and Pacifics with much lighter thrusts. As the V4s were new engines intended to be used mainly on relatively light duties there is little reason to suppose that there would have been dire trouble. It now appears that Darlington Works at least set valves on Gresley engines in the cold condition, not allowing for expansion. Optical lining up would doubtless have benefited the V4s as it did other Gresley types. The lighter connecting rods and motion of the V4s were easier to dismantle than the heavier B1 parts. The V4s would have been better riding and may well have given less trouble from vibration and cracked frames than the B1s. The V4s would have had a wider field of action in LNER days. Again it must be emphasised that the railway CME did not have to choose between perfection and failure: he had to choose between different methods of compromise.

There were certain points of detailed design in which the V4s differed from previous Gresley designs. Chief among them was the plainer type of valve spindle guide. This was the third variant of this item, the second appearing on the rear spindles of A3 No 2500 in 1934. Other differences were the square casings for the low outside steam pipes and the large dome with steam collector tail. A Gresley pattern pull-out regulator handle and a vertical screw reverser was provided as on the V2s, but maximum cut off was increased to 70 per cent instead of the usual 65 per cent on the V2s. In order to avoid a long movement of the reversing rod from full forward to full back gear with the short radius rod of the Walschaerts gear necessary as a result of the short wheelbase, the radius rod was lifted in front of the expansion link by a bell crank sliding between the built up expansion link, thus avoiding the use of the swinging suspension link and the valve errors due to die slip. This arrangement was also used on the P2s and later by Thompson on the A2s.

It is unfortunate that the V4s appeared too late, but this was over-shadowed by the major tragedy of world war. Had the V4s appeared earlier and had they been able to run for some years in a world at peace they might have established themselves in the same way as the V2, perhaps surpassing the larger engines in general utility.

CHAPTER TWELVE

The Gresley Big Engine Policy in Perspective

Now that the steam locomotive has vanished from commercial service on British main lines, it becomes possible to look back at history with clinical detachment. There have been a number of alternative locomotive policies in this country and each policy has produced its quota of successes and failures. It is inevitable that the supporters of each idea maintain that if only their own favourite schemes had been more fully implemented then steam would still be the prime mover in this country. It is unlikely that any such claim is true, but the conflicting viewpoints make interesting subjects for discussion. The Gresley regime is identified by the "big engine policy", which means that Gresley believed that economy could be obtained by using engines which were large for the daily tasks they had to perform. It was part of Gresley's basic faith that a double-headed train was a sign of failure and in this he continued the traditional policy of Stirling and Ivatt on the GNR. The P1, the P2 and the V2 were large locomotives for this country by any standard, while the V4 was a large engine for the work for which it was intended. They were all examples of the "big engine policy" put into practice and we may ask ourselves how real was the economy actually obtained.

It is certainly true that the greatest amount of work for the minimum amount of fuel was achieved when an engine was worked at something well below its maximum capacity. The many test house reports published since World War II confirm that this was the case for British simple locomotives. The French Chapelon compounds retained much of their economy even when pushed to very high rates of evaporation. The general conclusion for Britain, however, was that working an engine very hard for its size meant that it was burning coal at a disproportionately high rate and that maintenance costs also rose to an undesirable level. This could be accepted for one or two days each year, but it was not good operating to expect such hard work every day. The greatest economy was to be found by working engines at their optimum rates of evaporation and during the latter days of steam haulage some attempt was made to adjust schedules and loads to fit the engines. Gresley sought to build engines as large as the loading gauge would permit, but the operating people soon took advantage of the power available and finally even some of the large Gresley engines had to be extended to keep time on some jobs. The A4, for example, was bigger than was needed for the 230 ton "Silver Jubilee" of 1935, but by 1937 A4s were expected to run just as fast with the 325 ton "Coronation".

As far as the above argument goes Gresley was right in building his "big engines", but there was another side to the question. A big engine cost more to build and unless more work was obtained from it, capital had been misused. It may well have been that the LMS built 125 Black Fives for the cost of 100 V2s. If the average load hauled by each Black Five was just as heavy as that hauled by each V2 that was an advantage to the cheaper and smaller engine to be set against any reduced coal or maintenance costs. There was also the question, when a new very large engine was introduced, of how much money was needed to adapt the fixed installations on the railway to the new machines. Some of the expenses involved were new, longer turntables and alterations to such things as water columns which would not come over the new high tenders. Big engines took up more room in sheds and alongside station platforms, passenger trains based on the capacity of the engine might overlap station platforms, while freight trains might be too long for sidings. Clearly all was not economy when big engines were introduced.

The key question as to whether the building of big engines was justified was, of course, the decision of how many were to be built. If the correct number of big engines was built they could be used mainly on work beyond the capacity of smaller engines and they could save money by eliminating double-heading or the division of trains. A steam locomotive could easily last for thirty years and in thirty years traffic patterns would change. It was beyond human wisdom to choose the correct number of any class of engine and to expect the figure to be equally correct in thirty years time. In pre-war days the relatively small number of V2s could, generally speaking, be used on work worthy of the size of the engine. In wartime there was work for a larger number of V2s and some of the work would be beyond the powers of smaller engines. These conditions continued, to some extent, during the first few years of peace. At first the post-war world had petrol rationing and free road competition was not allowed, but as private motoring and the large scale use of lorries began to dominate national transport policy, the reduction in railway traffic meant that many V2s had to be used on work which was of such a trivial nature as to be more fitted for a 2-4-0, had any survived, than for a large 2-6-2.

If an engine was employed on work well below its optimum capacity it would become relatively uneconomical. Even if the figure of lbs of coal per mile seemed reasonably low the figure in terms of coal/dbhp/hr would be less favourable. This is all logical and predictable as an engine and tender, weighing 150 tons, hauling 200 tons, would need more power to move itself than to move its revenue-earning load. The test house results of the V2 as compared with those of the B1 suggest that it was the reverse of economical to employ a V2 when the work was well within the capacity of a B1. In wartime, however, it would have been impossible to have worked the 700 ton main-line expresses with success with the B1s or any other class of Class 5 4-6-0, but many post-war tasks of the V2s might have been handled more cheaply by the smaller engines.

Gresley believed in the wide firebox made possible by a pair of small carrying wheels at the rear of the locomotive. This was possible in the 4-6-2, 2-8-2 and 2-6-2 wheel arrangements that he used. It was claimed that the wide firebox allowed for the use of coal of poorer quality with less trouble than in the narrow firebox. It was also contended, with some justification, that the wide firebox was better for an engine used on a long continuous run such as the Kings Cross–Edinburgh nonstop. At first events seemed to give support to the wide firebox. During the 1926 coal strike the GWR "Castles", the victors of the 1925 Exchanges, lost much of their sparkle while the Gresley Pacifics managed increased loads of 600 tons with little trouble even with the imported fuel. It is also true that during the first few years of World War II the LNER appeared to have a considerable advantage over the other groups because of their large fleet of 4-6-2 and 2-6-2 engines. Perhaps the greatest compliment ever paid to the Gresley V2s came in 1942 when the LMS drawing office at Derby, under the leadership of the powerful personality of T. F. Coleman, prepared 12 proposed standard designs for post-war development. These included a 2-6-2 engine which could perhaps best be described as Derby's version of Doncaster's V2. A drawing and description of this engine can be found in *Chronicles of Steam* (Ian Allan, 1967). During the latter part of the war, however, coal and maintenance problems multiplied to such an extent that the wide firebox types suffered along with the rest. In fact it may even have been the case that the very success of the engines, earlier in the war, led to their undoing. The V2s and many of the Pacifics were so terribly abused during the final years of hostilities and the early years of peace that a smaller engine would not have remained operational at all.

It cannot be denied that some of the most impressive evaporation rates, in relation to the size of the boiler, have been obtained, both in this country and abroad, by narrow firebox engines. We do not know the exact figure for the evaporation rates of the LNWR "Georges" during the years 1910–1916 when they handled loads of 400–450 tons in everyday service on schedules of 55–57 mph along the main line from Euston to Crewe. In 1953 we have some evaporation rates from the re-draughted GWR "King" which were comparable with those from the bigger boilers of the V2 and the "Britannia". In France we had the most remarkable figures of all from the narrow firebox of the Chapelon 4-8-0. On the basis of these figures it would appear that the wide firebox does not mean a better boiler, but it does mean that there was room for the location of a bigger boiler. Some post-war French compounds with wide fireboxes equalled the Chapelon 4-8-0s in coal/dbhp/hr, but none of them equalled the 4-8-0s in power/weight ratio. It has been suggested that boiler maintenance costs were lower with the large wide firebox, but definite evidence is lacking. It can be said that European opinion, even including France, seemed to be moving in favour of the wide firebox when other forms of motive power ousted steam. Dogmatic conclusions should, however, be avoided as, since the end of steam in Europe, there have been some exciting experiments in South America which have not yet reached finality.

The bigger boiler, on an engine with a two- or four-wheeled trailing truck, was possible at the expense of adhesion weight. A lower proportion of the total weight of the engine rested on the driving wheels and there was the added problem of weight transference at starting. In the case of a 4-6-0 or a 4-8-0 any weight transference, under the influence of the drawbar pull at starting, meant more weight on the rear pair of coupled wheels. On the 4-6-2, 2-6-2 or 2-8-2 it meant more weight on the idle wheels which was no help to the starting ability of the engine. There is little doubt that a 4-6-0 was a better starter than a Pacific or a V2. This could be observed many times and in many places; a former GCR Class B7 4-6-0 would take a heavy train away from a station quicker than a

V2, while an SR Class S15 4-6-0 would make a more sure-footed start than a Bulleid Pacific. The bigger engine gained advantage from its bigger boiler in more dbhp at higher speeds.

The engine with a two-wheeled trailing truck gained advantages at high speed. This was because, in general, the idle wheels at the rear end of the engine made for a better riding machine at very high speeds. The larger boiler acted as thermal storage which could be added to when the engine was at rest or running easily and could be drawn upon if an exceptional effort was needed. The only engines in the world which have attained authentic maximum speeds of 120 mph or over have either two- or four-wheeled trailing trucks. Gresley engines held many of the British records for maximum and sustained high speeds. There is, however, little doubt that a 4-6-0 was a most useful engine for mixed traffic duties in Britain. A total of 75 per cent of the total weight of 4-6-0 was available for adhesion and this weight was not made any less effective by weight trans-ference at starting. While it would not fit the NBR loading gauge in height and width a GWR "King" would give almost the ideal curve of dbhp for the Edinburgh–Aberdeen road. It might have been possible to have built a large 4-6-0 which would have given more sure-footed starts than a Pacific or a V2. This is not to say that the 4-6-0 would rival the Pacific at high-speed service on the easy GNR main line. In the case of the 2-8-2s the 80 tons of adhesion weight made them more effective at starting up heavy grades than any Pacific, 2-6-2 or 4-6-0 but some expert writers consider that a 4-8-0 might have been better than a 2-8-2. A line drawing and description of such an engine was given by Dr Tuplin in the August 1958 issue of *Railways*. More recently it has been revealed that R. A. Riddles considers that the Class 6 Standard BR Pacifics, the "Clans", might have been a more effective engine for Scotland had they been built as 4-8-0s. This is discussed in more detail in *The Last Steam Locomotive Engineer* by Col. H. C. B. Rogers (Allen & Unwin, 1970).

In all questions of steam locomotive performance care has to be taken to avoid arguing from the particular to the general and it must be stated, as an established fact, that some of the greatest feats of hill-climbing ever recorded in Britain were to the credit of Pacific type locomotives. To take what is perhaps the most notable feat of all we find that the LMS "Duchess" class Pacific No 46225 exerted a dbhp of 2200 for half an hour at 30 mph when hauling the equivalent of 900 tons up a continuous grade of 1 in 100. It would however have been a most unsafe assumption that, because of this, a

"Duchess" would have been as reliable in uphill starting as the Gresley 2-8-2s because in regular daily service in all weathers, in normal operating conditions with one fireman. The "Duchesses", at times, lost time or had to take bankers, with loads far lower than 900 tons, owing to slipping on the northern banks. The SR "Merchant Navy" class Pacific, which had just as much steam available in its boiler as the "Duchess", could not be extended to anything like a maximum effort over Ais Gill because of the fear of slipping. By the same token it might have been possible for a sophisticated British 4-6-0 or 4-8-0 to have run the LNER "Coronation" or the BR "Elizabethan" with success under test conditions, but such an engine would have been unlikely to have fared better on the job under everyday running conditions than the Gresley A4s.

It must be realised that Gresley did not build the P1 or P2 2-8-2s for general service; they were built for specialised jobs. Even the V2s, which were regarded as mixed traffic engines, were first announced as "a new design for heavy long-distance work". As such they should be judged. Only the V4s were intended for general mixed traffic duty as the term was understood by the LMS. It is difficult to make dogmatic assertions about the V4s, for the design was never multiplied and they appeared too late for the duties for which they were intended. In wartime the need was to keep traffic moving while the V4s were intended for the acceleration of secondary services. In the idiom of the countryside, in the case of the V4s, the dog never saw the rabbit.

It has been questioned if the building of a small class of locomotives for a specific duty was ever justified financially. It is suggested that it was cheaper to double-head the few really heavy trains by two loco-motives of standard design. The LMS had a problem similar to that of the Edinburgh–Aberdeen road with its own "Royal Highlander" over the Perth–Inverness road, but they used two Stanier Black Fives. The desire for a single locomotive was present even in LMS thinking for they considered an express Garratt for this route and an illustration of such an engine appears in *Locomotive Panorama* Vol 1 by E. S. Cox (Ian Allan, 1965). The LMS problem was more seasonal than the "Aberdonian" in the mid-1930s. It is probable that, had the Highland been included in the LNER group, Gresley would have pushed forward with the designing of a suitable big engine.

It has been said that the test of success is shown by the degree to which others are willing to imitate. There was a distinct movement towards the Gresley "big engine" policy in Britain. It is perhaps not surprising that Bulleid, who was Gresley's second in command and powerful advocate of some of his ideas, should introduce a similar policy on the SR. At first he hoped to build a 4-8-2, then a 2-8-2, for express services on the SR but opposition from the Civil Engineer caused this to be changed to a Pacific, corresponding to an A4 rather than to a P2. Bulleid built large numbers of "West Country" and "Battle of Britain" Class Pacifics which were, at least, the equals of any V2 in maximum power output under optimum conditions. They had a much wider route availability than a V2, but they were more addicted to slipping because of their reduced adhesion weight. The GWR remained faithful to the 4-6-0, while the LMS sought compromise by building Pacifics for the heaviest expresses but retaining 4-6-0s for general duties. The BR standard range seemed at first to be a vindication of Gresley's ideas of big boilers and wide fireboxes, but there was some retreat when the proposed Class 5 Pacific was rejected in favour of a 4-6-0.

As this is a book about Gresley locomotives the defects of his engines have, perforce, been emphasised. It would, however, be wrong to think that troubles afflicted the Gresley engines alone while rival designers produced machines of immaculate performance. The Gresley conjugate valve gear, for example, gave uneven cylinder hp outputs at some speeds, but the aficionados of other railways should not become too pious about this. Certainly more hp was developed by the inside cylinder of a Gresley three-cylinder engine with the 2 and 1 gear and some very queer indicator diagrams were produced by the V2 at Swindon, but it would be a great mistake to think that there was always perfectly even steam distribution in the cylinders of non-Gresley locomotives. The steam locomotive, much as it was to be admired, was never a machine of great precision. There was often considerable difference in the hps developed in the cylinders of two- and four-cylindered engines and in three-cylindered engines with separate sets of valve gear while, at times, the forward and backward strokes of the piston in the same cylinder gave different hps. At one time it was found that there was a difference of over an inch in the internal diameter of the two cylinders of one of the GCR Atlantics stationed at Leicester shed. The engine had never shown any inclination to veer off into the fields and it had tackled some quite hard jobs, for its size, apparently just as well as its stable mates. If such a picture horrifies the purists then they should think for a moment about the number of times when differences in valve setting between right and left cylinders must have brought about differences in hps quite as great as the inch in diameter. Unequal carbonisation around the valves and ports may have had similar results. The steam locomotive could and frequently did run well when there was little of the precision demanded by more sophistic-ated forms of motive power. It is against such a background that the vagaries of the Gresley engines with their 2 and 1 gear should be considered.

The gear was by no means ideal, but other attempts to build high powered multi-cylindered engines, within our restricted loading gauge, had to face problems of their own. Inside eccentrics caused trouble from overheating and some inside sets of gear were placed in positions of monumental inaccessibility. Despite their theoretical shortcomings the Gresley engines, during the years 1935–1939, worked the fastest long-distance express passenger and freight trains in the land, held the British record for sustained high speed, in 1938 attained the world record maximum speed, hauled trains in peace-time as heavy as any in the land and during the first few years of war worked the heaviest passenger trains of all. This was all achieved on coal/dbhp/hr figures comparable with the best of their con-temporaries. It is true that they ran best under conditions of careful maintenance, but the best performance was never obtained any-where by neglect. Partisans who gloat over *Mallard*'s over-heated big end should proceed with restraint lest those who really know the truth reveal the inside story of certain epic runs on other railways.

Gresley has been criticised for not producing a full range of standard modern locomotives for the LNER in the Churchward manner or for not emulating Stanier's "mighty re-stocking" of the LMS, but the LNER was never a wealthy railway and there was little Gresley could do with the money available but top up the locomotive stock with new engines while keeping the aging designs fully operational. Despite all difficulties the LNER train services compared well with the best in the land. Gresley was never one to linger long in the gateway of indecision; he pressed on to the road beyond. It may be said that, at times, he did this when a slight pause for consolidation might have helped. There could be some valid criticisms of Doncaster's reluctance to make small modifications to existing designs, although the running shed people knew how badly they were needed. Small but vital improvements were made to the V2s, for example, almost at the eleventh hour for steam. The knowledge had been there earlier. Yet there remains much to be admired in Gresley's breadth of vision; no one in his empire would have called a Fowler Class 4 0-6-0 "The Big Goods". At the outbreak of war Gresley was looking ahead to a peacetime railway with an elite corps of very high-speed expresses worked by A4s and Super A4s, very heavy ordinary expresses worked to smart inter-mediate timings by 4-8-2s derived from the P2 design, and the fastest fitted freight services in the land worked by V2s which would also have shared the secondary main line work and holiday specials with the older Pacifics. No British railway would have had a more potent second eleven. The bulk of the secondary and branch line services, on accelerated timings, would have been in the hands of the V4s while 2-6-4 tank engine versions of these would have handled improved suburban and short distance services. Such a vision showed the "big engine policy" fully implemented and it was, by no means, a dishonourable aim. Had peace remained the LNER might have come close to fulfilment.

Appendices

P1 CLASS

2393 built 7/25 rebuilt P1/2 11/42 withdrawn 7/45
2394 built 11/25 rebuilt P1/2 1/42 withdrawn 7/45

P2 CLASS

No	Class	Built	Rebuilt as P2/2	Rebuilt as A2/2	Withdrawn
2001	P2/1	5/34	4/38	7/44	2/60
2002	P2/2	10/34		8/44	17/61
2003	P2/2	6/36		12/44	11/59
2004	P2/2	7/36		10/44	1/61
2005	P2/2	8/36		1/43	11/59
2006	P2/3	9/36		4/44	3/61

No 2002 was given a streamlined nose to conform with 2003–6 on 10/36. 2001 on 4/38. No 2005 was fitted with single Kylchap blast-pipe with no difference in classification. It was converted to A2, later A2/2, with double Kylchap. No 2006 built with modified boiler with combustion chamber Type 108, hence different classification P2/3. No 2004 fitted with exhaust bypass valve but no different classification.

V2 CLASS

First engine built 20/6/36

Batches:—

4771-5	Doncaster	1936
4776-95	Darlington	1937
4796-4814	Darlington	1938
4815-42	Darlington	1939
4843-46	Doncaster	1939
4847-52	Doncaster	1940
4853-62	Darlington	1939
4863-88	Darlington	1940
4889-98	Darlington	1941
4899	Darlington	1942

3641-54	Darlington	1942
3655-60	Doncaster	1941
3661-4	Doncaster	1942
3665-74	Darlington	1942
3675-90	Darlington	1943
3691-5	Darlington	1944

First engine withdrawn	26/2/1962
Last engine withdrawn	31/12/1966

V4 Class

	Built	*Withdrawn*
3401	2/41	3/57
3402	3/41	11/57

NUMBERS

P1 Class

2393/4

Under the 1943 LNER re-numbering scheme these engines were intended to be 3990/1 but they were withdrawn before the scheme was implemented.

P2 Class

2001–2006   re-numbered 501–506, BR 60501–6

The original intention was to number *Cock o' the North* 2981 and this number was stamped on the motion. This was changed to 2001, which was the number of the first passenger 4-6-0 built by the NER in 1899. Re-numbering took place after the engines were rebuilt as A2/2 class Pacifics, but the original intention was for these engines to have been numbered 990–995. This would have meant that the number of the first British passenger 4-6-0 would have changed to the number of Britain's first Atlantic.

V2 Class

Green Arrow was originally intended to be No 637.
4771–4899   re-numbered   800-938, BR 60800-60938
3641–3695   re-numbered   939-983, BR 60939-60983

In the original 1943 scheme the V2s would have become 700–883 and nineteen engines received these numbers before the 1946 scheme came into effect. These were—701, 710, 711, 714, 718–722, 729, 733,

750, 762, 771, 795, 799, 805, 809, and 871. Under BR 60000 was added to all LNER numbers from 3/48 onwards.

V4 Class

3401/2   re-numbered 1700/1 BR 61700/1

NAMES

P2 Class

2001	*Cock o' the North*	The provocative nickname of a former chief of Clan Gordon. Thought by many to contain a note of challenge by Gresley.
2002	*Earl Marischal*	The title of the President of the Scottish College of Heralds.
2003	*Lord President*	The presiding judge of the Scottish Court of Session.
2004	*Mons Meg*	The nickname of an ancient piece of artillery preserved at Edinburgh Castle.
2005	*Thane of Fife*	The title of the Lord of the Ancient Scottish kingdom of Fife made generally famous by Shakespeare in "Macbeth".
2006	*Wolf of Badenoch*	The nickname of a former Earl of Buchan who was a cruel and ruthless leader of raiding parties. The Scottish equivalent of a Wild West "Bad-man".

All the P2s had straight nameplates on the sides of the smokebox.

V2 Class

4771	*Green Arrow*	6/36 when built
4780	*The Snapper*	11/9/1937
	The East Yorkshire Regiment— The Duke of York's Own	
4806	*The Green Howard*	24/9/1938
	Alexandra, Princess of Wales's Own Yorkshire Regiment	
4818	*St Peter's School York AD 627*	
4831	*Durham School*	3/4/1939
4843	*The King's Own Yorkshire Light Infantry*	15/6/1939
		20/5 1939

4844   *The Coldstreamer*   20/6/1939
60964 *The Durham Light Infantry*   29/4/1958

Green Arrow had straight nameplates on the smokebox sides, but the original intention was to use curved nameplates with dummy splashers. A photograph of the engine as No 637 with such nameplates exists. This arrangement was apparently not liked, but it had to be used in the case of the regimental names with their very long titles.

V4 Class

3401   *Bantam Cock*   A farmyard bird noted for being strong and aggressive for its size.

PRESERVATION

Green Arrow has been restored to LNER green and re-numbered 4771. It has been stored at Leicester Midland shed, moved to Preston Park and is now at Norwich. It is to be hoped that various rumours now circulating about the chances of it being used for running specials come to a happy state of confirmation.

ALLOCATIONS

P1

The P1s spent their entire existence at New England shed.

P2s

Apart from test running on the GNR main line from Doncaster shed and a short stay at Kings Cross for test running in the early days of 2001, the P2s spent their whole time working from

Haymarket	2001/4
Dundee	2003/5
Aberdeen	2002/6

V2s

The V2s were limited in their range of action by their route availability. The distribution pattern can be indicated by the following tables showing the position as at 1/1/47 and again ten years later.

1947		1957	
Kings Cross	18	Kings Cross	14
New England	37	New England	21
Doncaster	20	Grantham	3
Sheffield	4	Doncaster	19
Gorton	4	Neasden	2
York	28	Woodford Halse	4
Darlington	2	Leicester	2
Gateshead	25	March	5
Heaton	12	York	26
Haymarket	14	Gateshead	15
Dundee	8	Heaton	18
Ferryhill	8	Tweedmouth	4
St Margarets	3	Ardsley	4
On loan		Copley Hill	4
Copley Hill	1	St Margarets	16
		Haymarket	5
		Dundee	11
		Ferryhill	11

The axle loading did not allow the V2s a very wide sphere of activity off their own main lines. The most interesting wanderings took place in 1953 when there was trouble on the Southern leading to the temporary withdrawal of a number of "Merchant Navy" class Pacifics. Help was given by engines from other regions, including a number of Class V2 engines which were employed on express services over the former LSWR main line. This included some running on the "Bournemouth Belle", a log of which was published by Cecil J. Allen. The V2 was not unduly vigorous in getting away and uphill, but it reached 86 mph on the descent past Winchester and recovered the slight loss of time. During the 1960s V2s were observed on specials on the Midland main line both north and south of Leicester. They reached GWR territory, from the GCR, at Banbury.

V4s

No 3401 started life with trial running from Doncaster shed after which it moved to the GE section. No 3402 was sent straight to Scotland and was joined by 3401. After trial running from Haymarket shed they both settled at Eastfield for work on the West Highland. In 1954 they were transferred to Aberdeen and were withdrawn from that shed. Had the class been multiplied they would doubtless have been seen almost everywhere.

TANK ENGINES

There has been no mention of the Gresley V1 and V3 tank engine classes in this book. A 2-6-2 tank engine is the equivalent of a 2-6-0 tender engine. The V1 and the V3 had the typical Gresley arrangement of three cylinders with the 2 and 1 gear. On outer suburban duties on the GER they got away no quicker from stops than the 4-4-0 "Claud Hamilton" class with 7 ft driving wheels, but equally showed no inferiority in speed when well away. This followed the Gresley tradition. A design for a 2-8-2 mineral tank engine for use from Colwick shed was prepared. This would have had a boiler similar to the 2-6-2Ts, but the design was abandoned owing to the decline in the coal trade. There were also doubts about the efficacy of braking on mineral tank engines.

UNFULFILLED PROJECTS

In 1938 plans were prepared, at least in general outline, for a main-line 4-8-2 express engine based on the P2 class but with 6 ft 8 in driving wheels. The design would have included a boiler which was based on that used on P2 No 2006 and on the rebuilt No 10000. It had the same 1 ft long combustion chamber, but it retained the 19 ft long barrel as in the earlier P2s. The design as illustrated in B. Spencer's paper and repeated in F. A. S. Brown's biography of Sir Nigel Gresley (Ian Allan, 1961) does not inspire much confidence, but the drawing most likely represented an early stage in planning. The worst fault is the extension of the boiler further into the cab than was the case with the P2s or the Pacifics. This would have meant a most uncomfortable cab for the driver, with an almost impossible firing position for the fireman. The Unions would certainly have been justified in calling for bonus payments for the crews of such engines. It may also be asked if a hand-fired 4-8-2 would ever have allowed for the potentialities of the type to be realised. The design was at least a realisation that Pacifics were not ideal engines for getting away and that limited loads or larger engines would be needed for the accelerated trains that were expected in the 1940s had there been peace.

There were also plans for a 2-6-4 tank engine equivalent to the V4s. This would have been unique in British practice since the GER Decapod for it was to be a tank engine with a wide firebox. Two alternative designs were prepared, one with three cylinders as with the V4s but with rather limited tank capacity due to the restriction in width past the wide firebox, and a two-cylinder design with an additional tank between the frames. It would be interesting to know just how much the two-cylinder design owed to a school of thought lobbying for greater simplicity, or whether it was a case of two cylinders having to be accepted as cruel necessity in order to locate the extra tank.

There were rumours at various times of other unfulfilled designs and while the P2s were being designed there were rumours of a 4-8-2 just as a 2-6-2 had been forecast as 1470 was being prepared in 1922. It is to be hoped that more revelations from the Doncaster archives are still to be published and we await the RCTS book on LNER locomotives with impatience.

LOAD LIMITS
P1 CLASS

At first these engines were in a special class allowed loads of 100 wagons, but this had to be reduced, as a matter of operating convenience, to 92 wagons. In practice, as the coal trade declined, P1 loads often were no greater than the 80 wagons allowed the 2-8-0s. In 1924 a new loading scheme was introduced by the LNER in the hope that it would supersede the varied methods of the old companies. In practice this did not work and the GNR J6s, for example, remained "A Engines" until the end of the chapter. The LNER power classification was never as rigidly applied as the LMS power classification which it resembled. After the removal of boosters the P1s were classified as Class 8 along with the larger 2-8-0s, but they were re-classified 9 when they were rebuilt with A3 type boilers and classed P1/2. It is doubtful if a class of only two engines could often have been limited to the heaviest loads in wartime conditions.

P2 CLASS

Loads for these engines were limited as much by operating convenience as by the power of the locomotives. The limits were:

Edinburgh–Dundee and return	550 tons
Dundee–Aberdeen and return	530 tons

These loads were 80–100 tons more than those allowed for the Pacifics and V2s.

V2 CLASS

On the GNR section there seem to have been few loading restrictions enforced on the Pacifics or V2s before the war and pilots were only seen in emergencies. On the NER section Pacifics and V2s sometimes took pilots in pre-war days with loads rather less than those worked successfully by unaided engines on the GNR. On the GCR the LNER loading for a V2 was 13 bogies, but this was influenced by restrictions on passenger trains entering Marylebone station. Long trains stopped movements at the station when vehicles were standing on track circuits and "locking the signalman up". On specials running to Wembley some very long trains were worked by V2s as when No 4796 took a 17 coach train up to Wembley via High Wycombe. The empty stock was then taken to Neasden sidings without infringing the Marylebone restrictions.

In Scotland the V2s shared the load limits of the Pacifics.

Edinburgh–Dundee	480 tons northbound	450 tons southbound
Dundee–Aberdeen	480 tons northbound	420 tons southbound
Edinburgh–Carlisle (Waverley route)	400 tons	

During the war there appear to have been few limits on loads over the GNR section during the first two years, but pilots were sometimes used on the NER. Later the limits fell to 20 bogies on the GNR, then to 18 and after the accelerations of 1945, 15 bogies were rarely exceeded.

On the GCR the Newcastle to Ashford trains run mainly for servicemen loaded, at times, to 21 bogies. A V2 was observed piloted by a GN Atlantic working a 20 coach load between Sheffield and Nottingham in 1942.

In BR days the V2s were classified 7P6F. The Class 7 passenger loading put the V2s in the same class as the "Royal Scots" and on the GCR both classes were allowed 450 tons.

The Class 6 loading was for loose-coupled freight trains but for fully fitted freights of Class C there was an additional allowance of 5 wagons.

GN SECTION

London to Doncaster	65 wagons
Doncaster to York	55 wagons
Grimsby to Peterborough	65 wagons

GC SECTION

Marylebone–Manchester	45 wagons
Woodford–Banbury	50 wagons
Banbury–Woodford	45 wagons

V4 Class

The V4 class were power class 5 in the 1949 list but they were derated to Class 4 in 1953. On the West Highland line they were allowed 250 tons against 300 for the K4 class 2-6-0s specially designed for the route.

Leading Dimensions

Class	P1	P1/1	P2/1	P2/2	P2/3	V2	V4
Cylinders (3)	20 × 26	19 × 26	21 × 26	21 × 26	21 × 26	18½ × 26	15 × 26
Driving wheel diameter	5 ft 2 in	5 ft 2 in	6 ft 2 in	6 ft 2 in	6 ft 2 in	6 ft 2 in	5 ft 8 in
Boiler pressure	180 lb	220 lb	220 lb	220 lb	220 lb	220 lb	250 lb
Heating surface							
Tubes	2715 sq ft	2477 sq ft	2477 sq ft	2477 sq ft	2345 sq ft	2216 sq ft	1292 sq ft
Firebox	215 sq ft	215 sq ft	237 sq ft	237 sq ft	253 sq ft	215 sq ft	151 sq ft
Superheater	525 sq ft	703 sq ft	777 sq ft	777 sq ft	749 sq ft	680 sq ft	356 sq ft
Grate Area	41.2 sq ft	41.2 sq ft	50 sq ft	50 sq ft	50 sq ft	41.2 sq ft	28.5 sq ft
Tractive Effort	38500 lb	42465 lb	43460 lb	43460 lb	43460 lb	33730 lb	27420 lb
With Booster	47000 lb	—	—	—	—	—	—
Weight in working order							
Engine	100 tons	92 tons	110 tons	107 tons	107 tons	93 tons	70 tons
Tender	51 tons	51 tons	55 tons	58 tons	58 tons	51 tons	43 tons

Bibliography

The Development of LNER Locomotive Design 1923–1941, B. Spencer. Paper read to The Institution of Locomotive Engineers, August 1947. Reprinted by RCTS, 1947.
Locomotives of the LNER, K. Prentice and P. Proud. RCTS, 1941.
The Steam Lcomotive in America, W. J. Bruce. W. W. Norton & Co., 1952.
Locomotive Performance and Efficiency Test Bulletin No 8 E & NE Region, the V2 class. BTC, 1954.
Nigel Gresley Locomotive Engineer, F. A. S. Brown. Ian Allan, 1961.
Master Builders of Steam, H. A. V. Bulleid. Ian Allan, 1963.
Locomotives of the LNER, A Preliminary Survey, Part 1, RCTS, 1963.
British Pacific Locomotives, C. J. Allen. Ian Allan, 1962.
Locomotive Panorama, E. S. Cox, Vol. 2, Ian Allan, 1966.
Chronicles of Steam, E. S. Cox. Ian Allan, 1967.
The Engines That Passed, C. Hamilton Ellis. Allen & Unwin, 1966.
World Steam in the 20th Century, E. S. Co. Ian Allan, 1969.
British Steam Since 1900, W. A. Tuplin. David & Charles, 1969.
The Last Steam Locomotive Engineer, R. A. Riddles, C. B. Rogers. Allen & Unwin, 1970.
Essays in Steam, SLS Anthology. Ian Allan, 1970.
The London and North Eastern Railway, C. J. Allen. Ian Allan, 1966.
Bill Hoole, Engineman Extraordinary, P. W. B. Semmens. Ian Allan, 1965.
On Engines in Britain and France, P. Ransome-Wallis. Ian Allan, 1957.

Various Issues of:
Railway Magazine, Railways, Railway World, Trains Illustrated, Modern Railways, The Railway Observer, The Journal of The Stephenson Locomotive Society, The Gresley Observer.

THE REBUILDS

A detailed coverage of the fortunes of the P2 class engines after rebuilding as Class A2/2 Pacifics and the record of engines Nos 3696–9, originally intended to be V2s but which were completed as smaller editions of the P2 rebuilds and were classified A2/1, lies outside the scope of this book. The story can be read in the following books.

British Pacific Locomotives, C. J. Allen. Ian Allan, 1962.
Essays in Steam, From Cock o' the North to St Johnstoun, P. J. Coster. Ian Allan, 1970.
Edward Thompson of the LNER, P. Grafton. Kestrel Books, 1971.